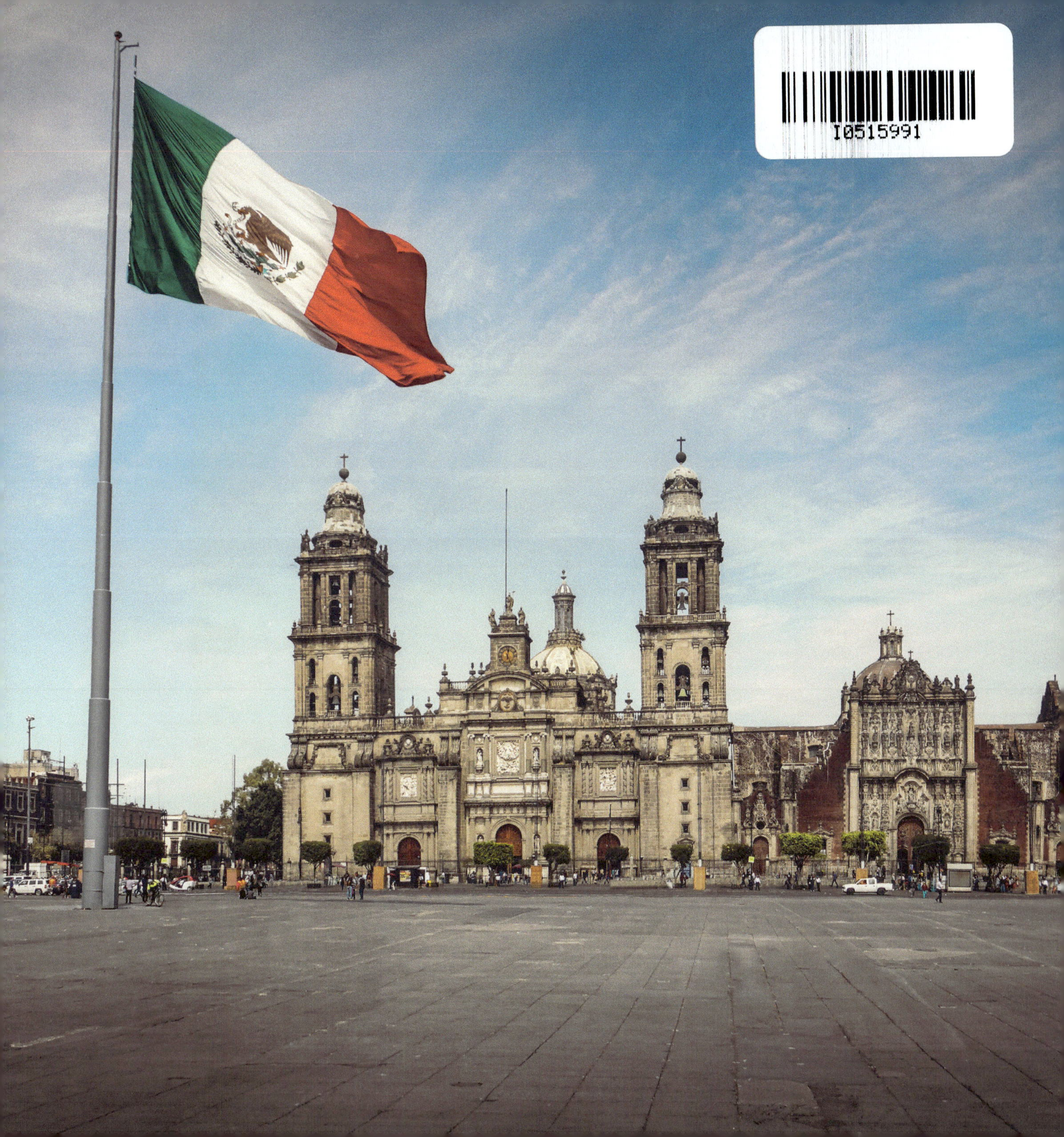

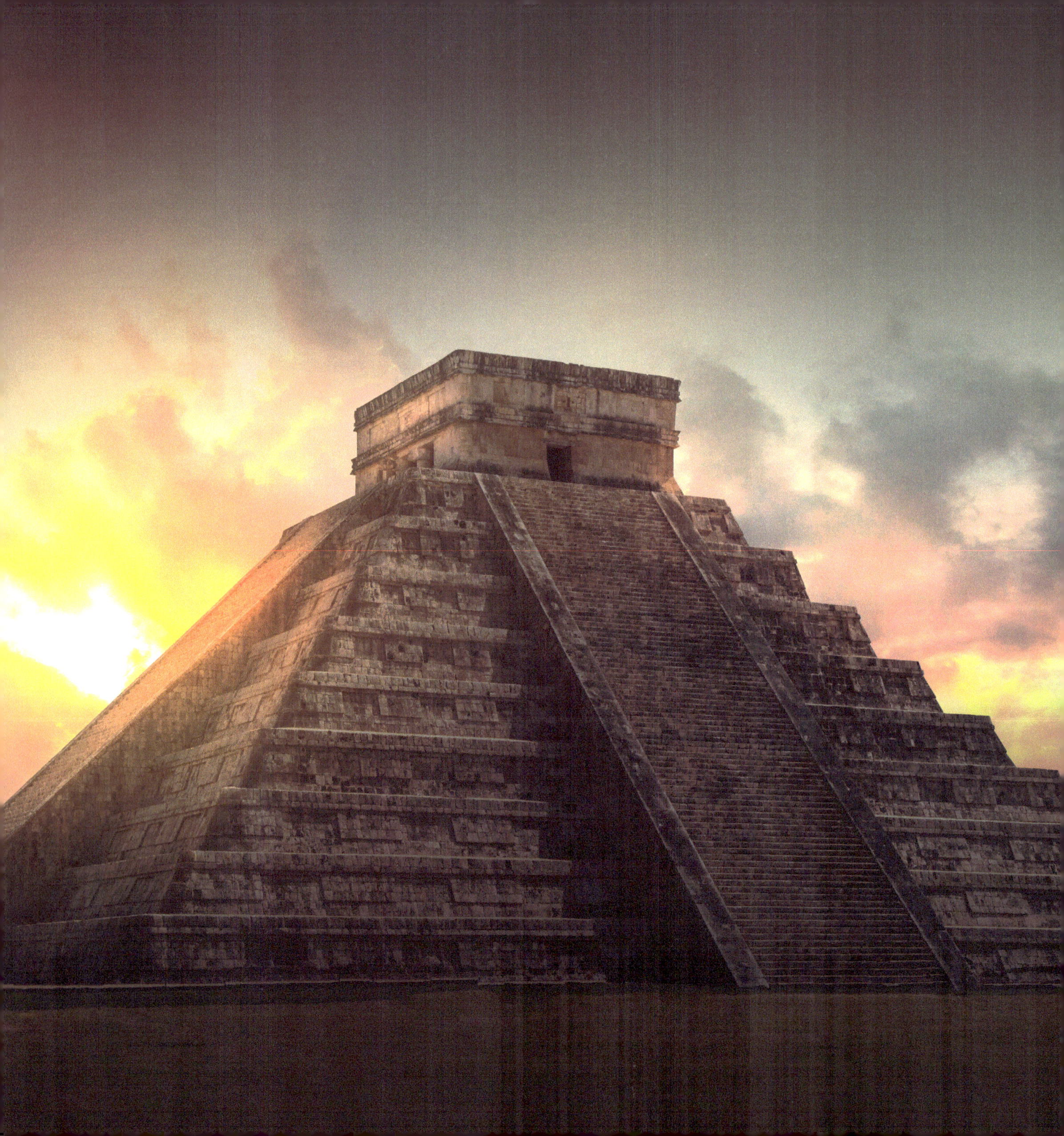

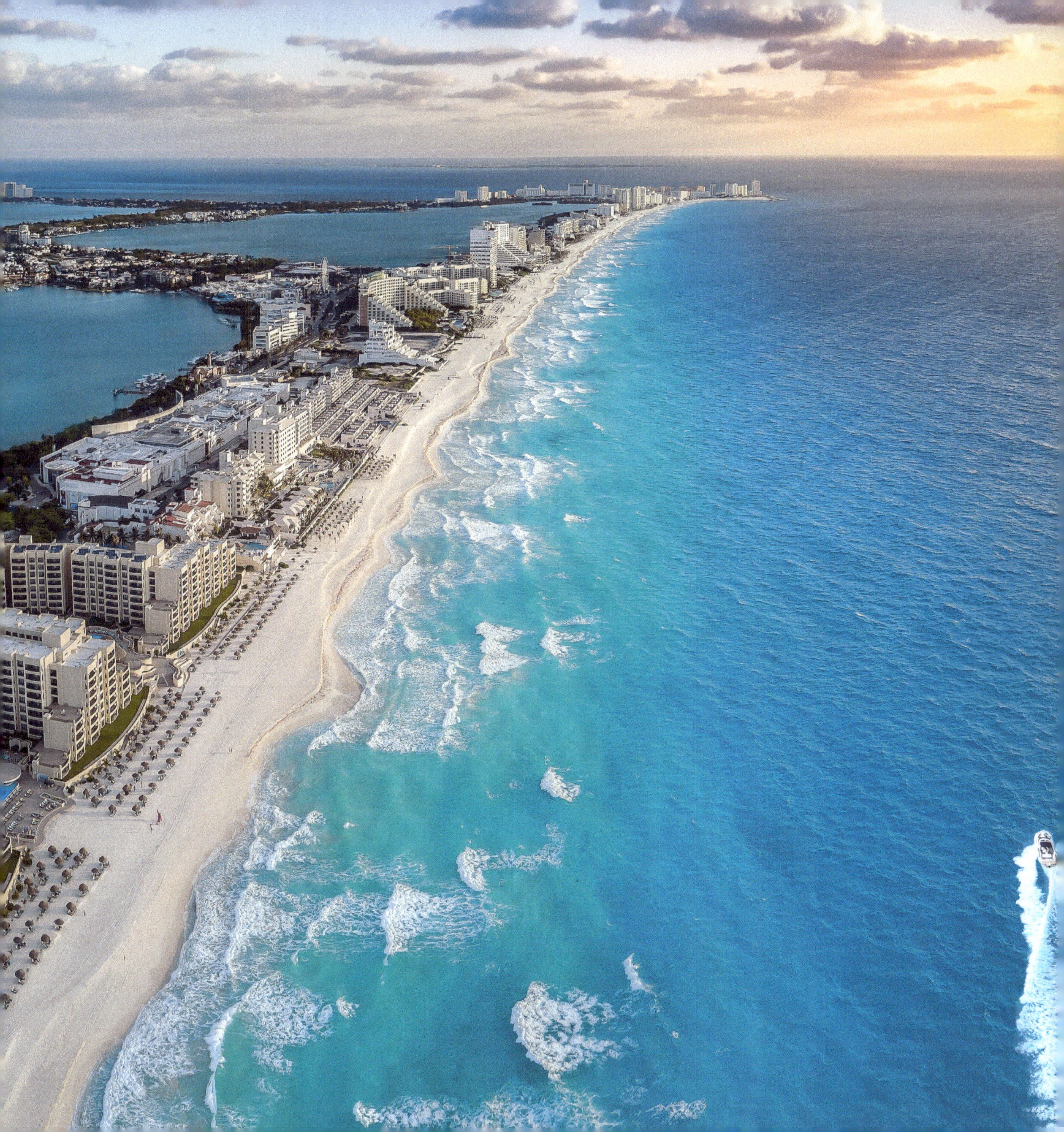

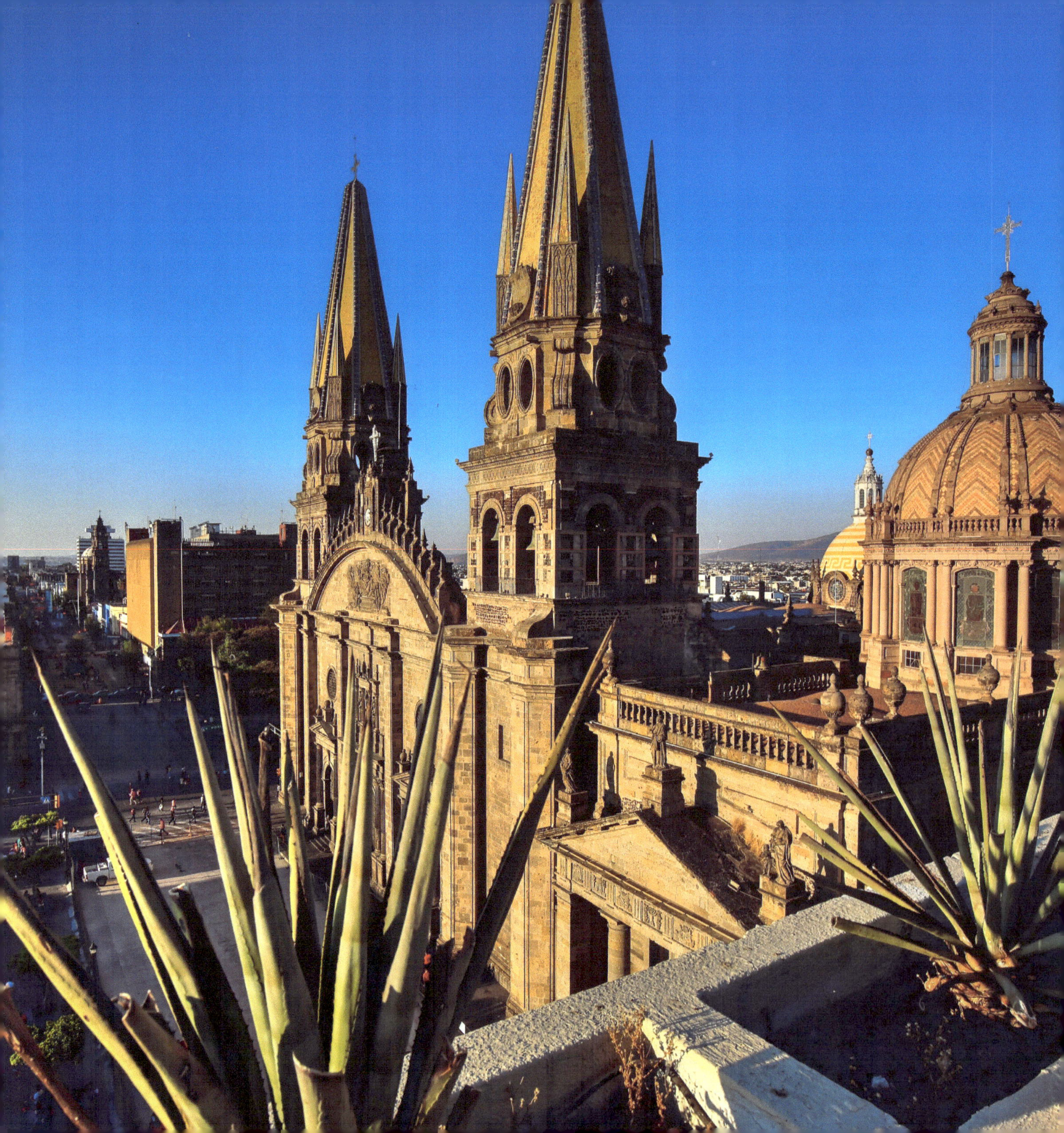

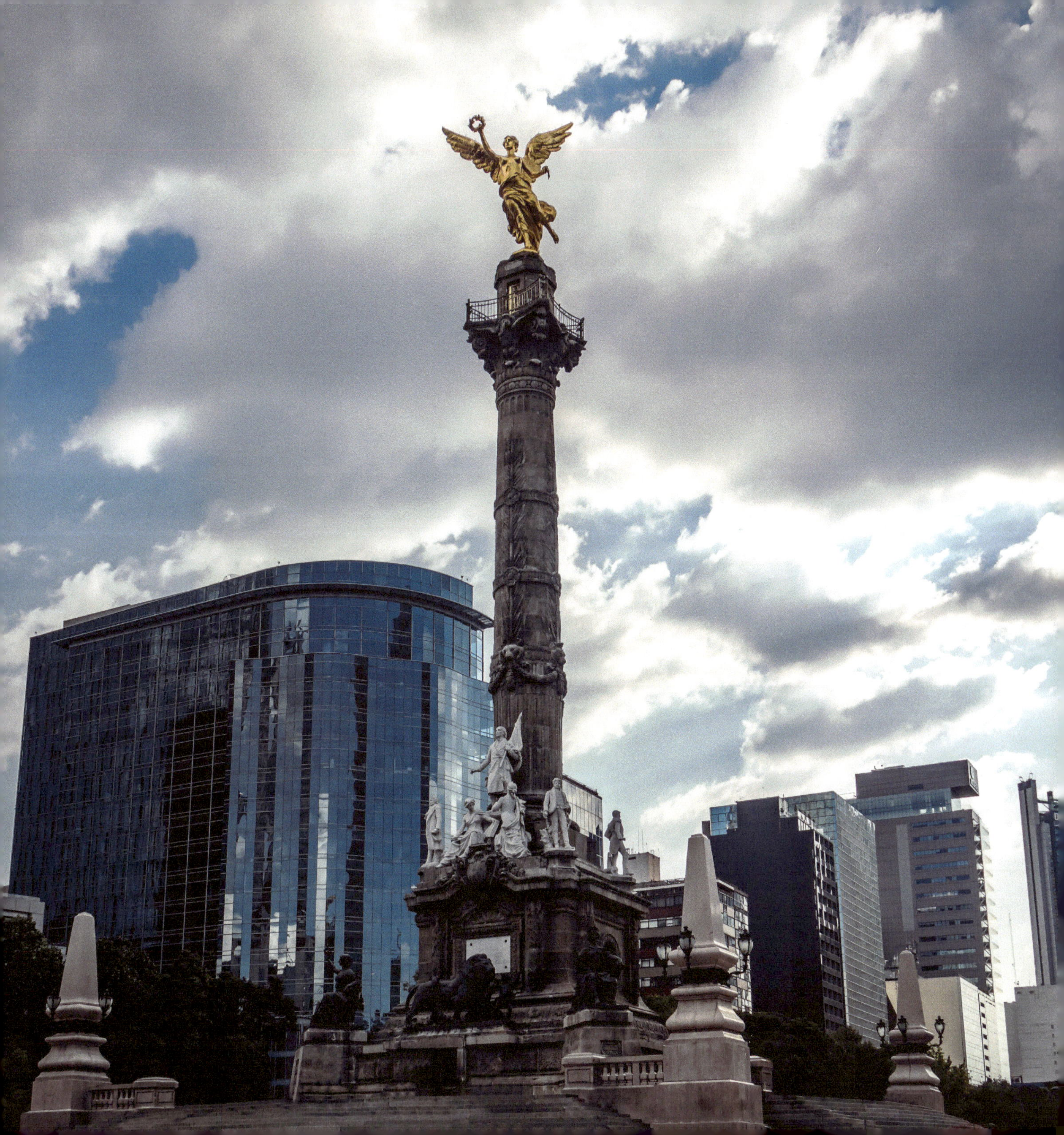

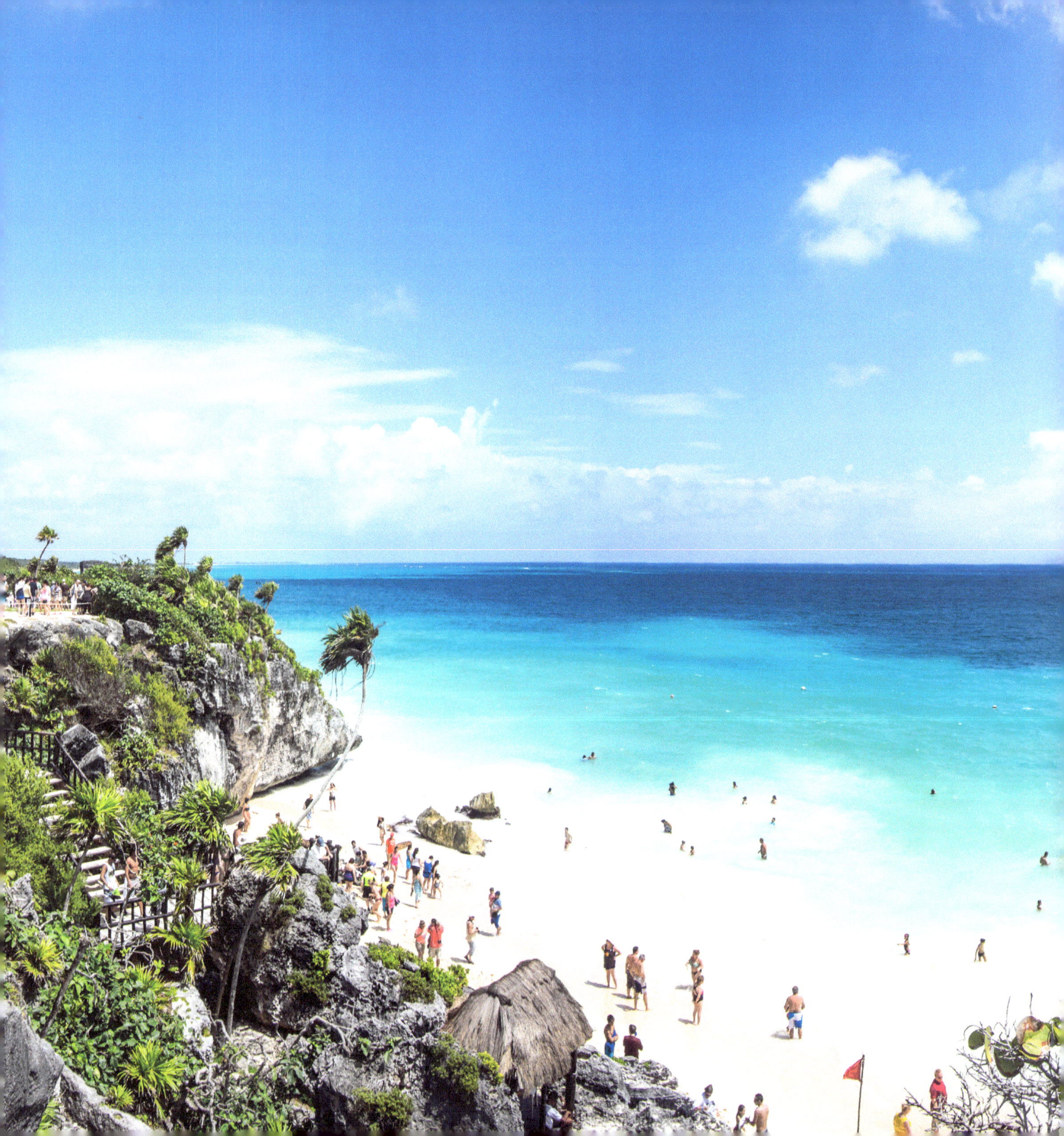

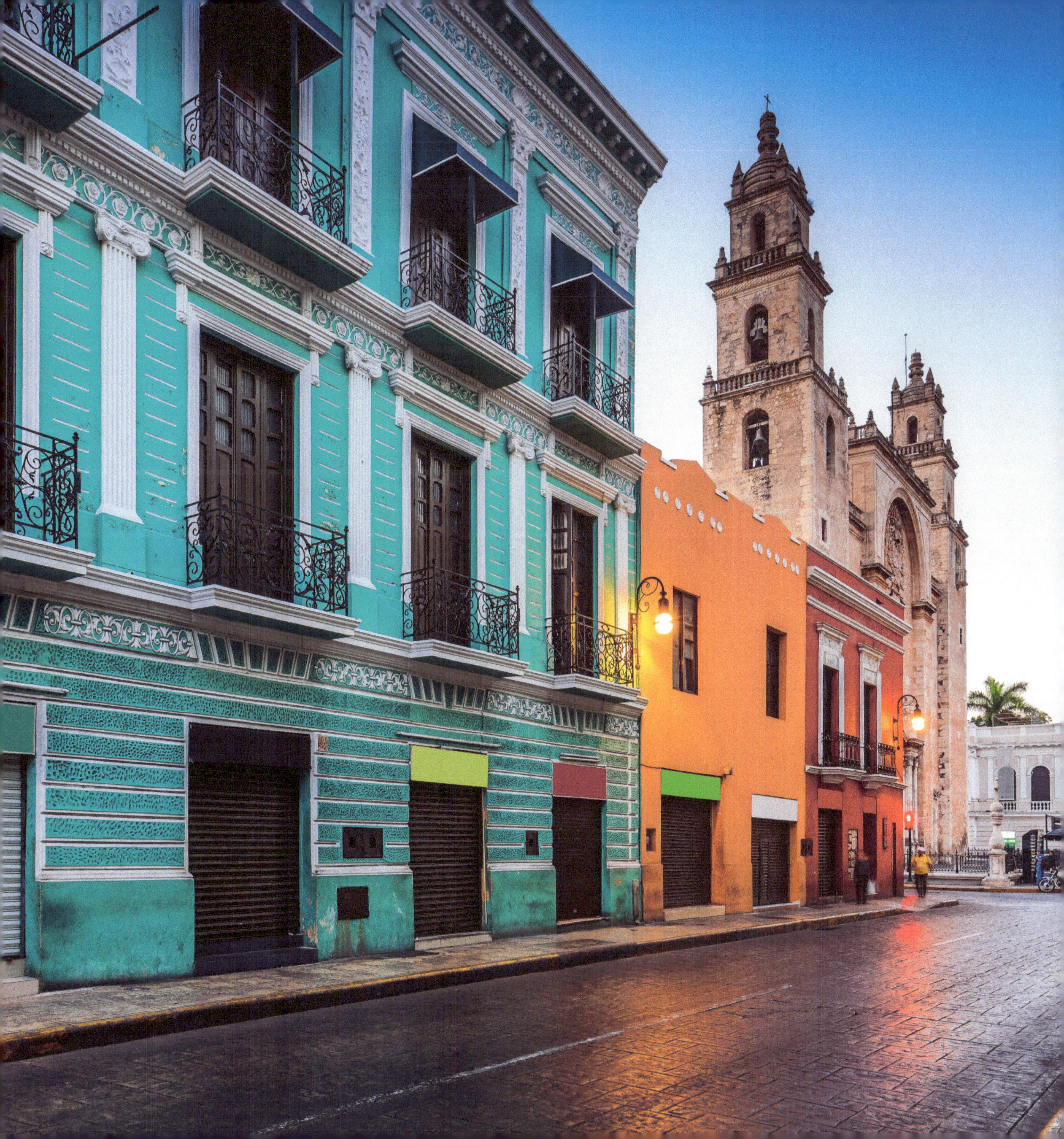

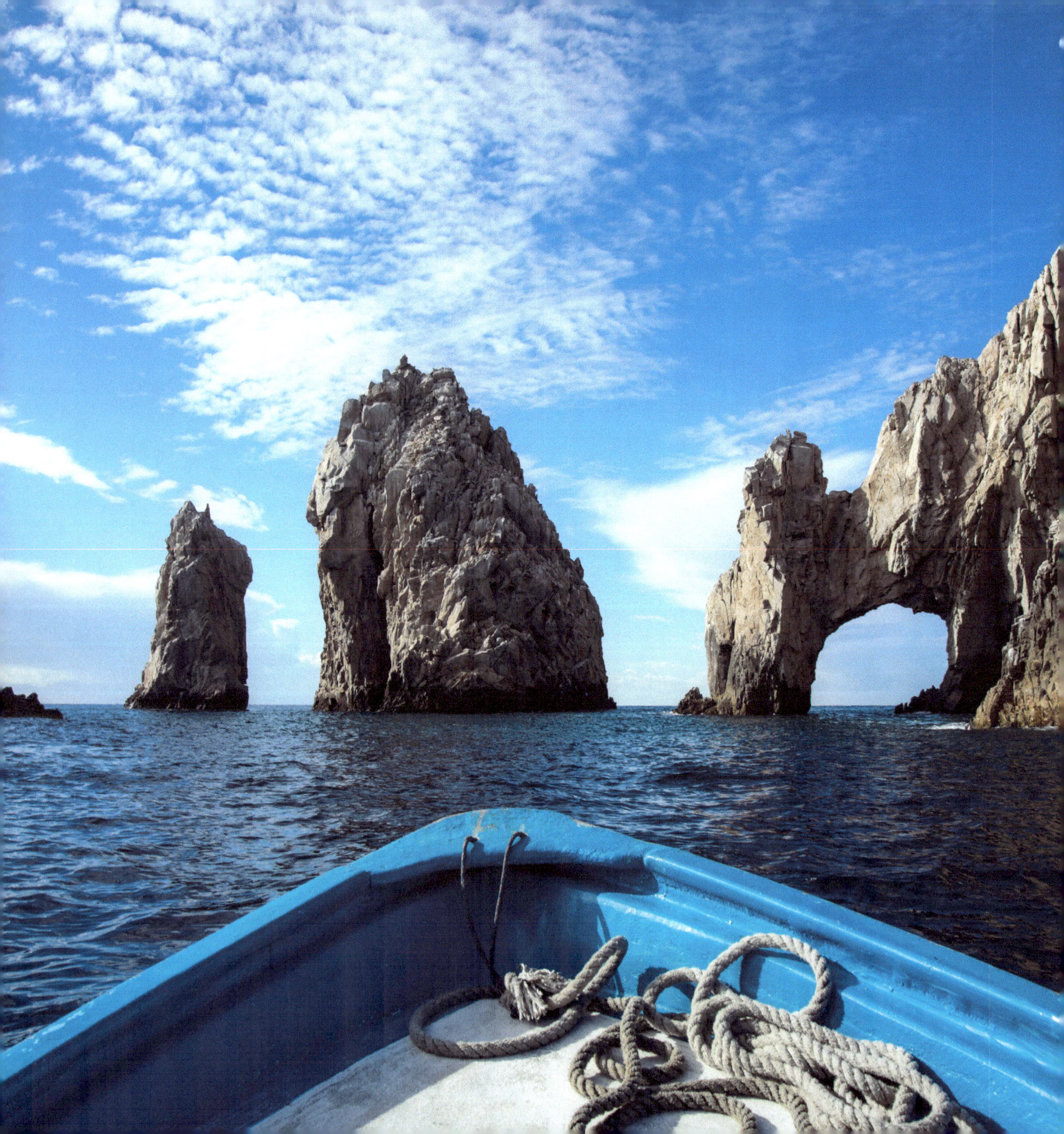

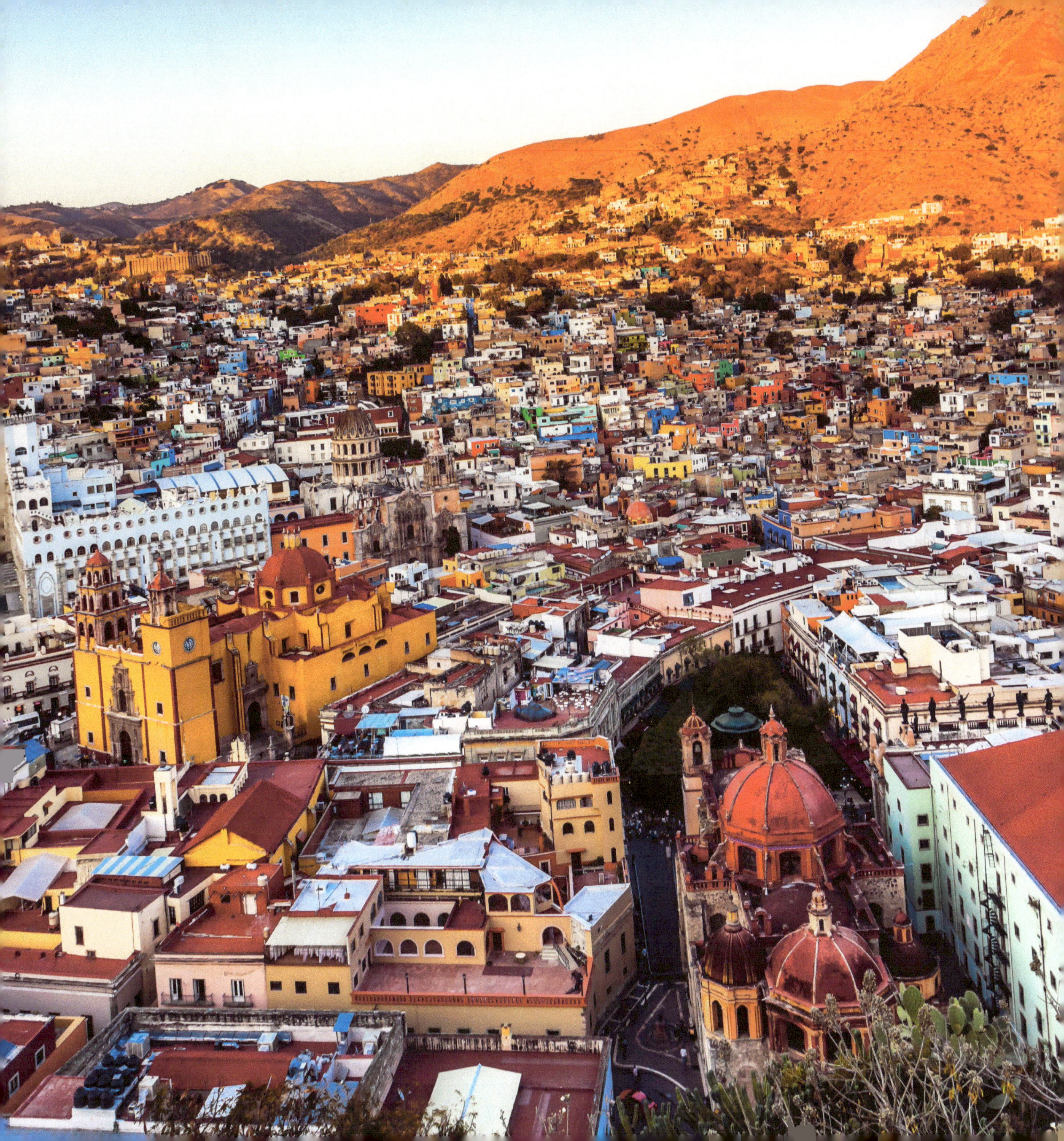

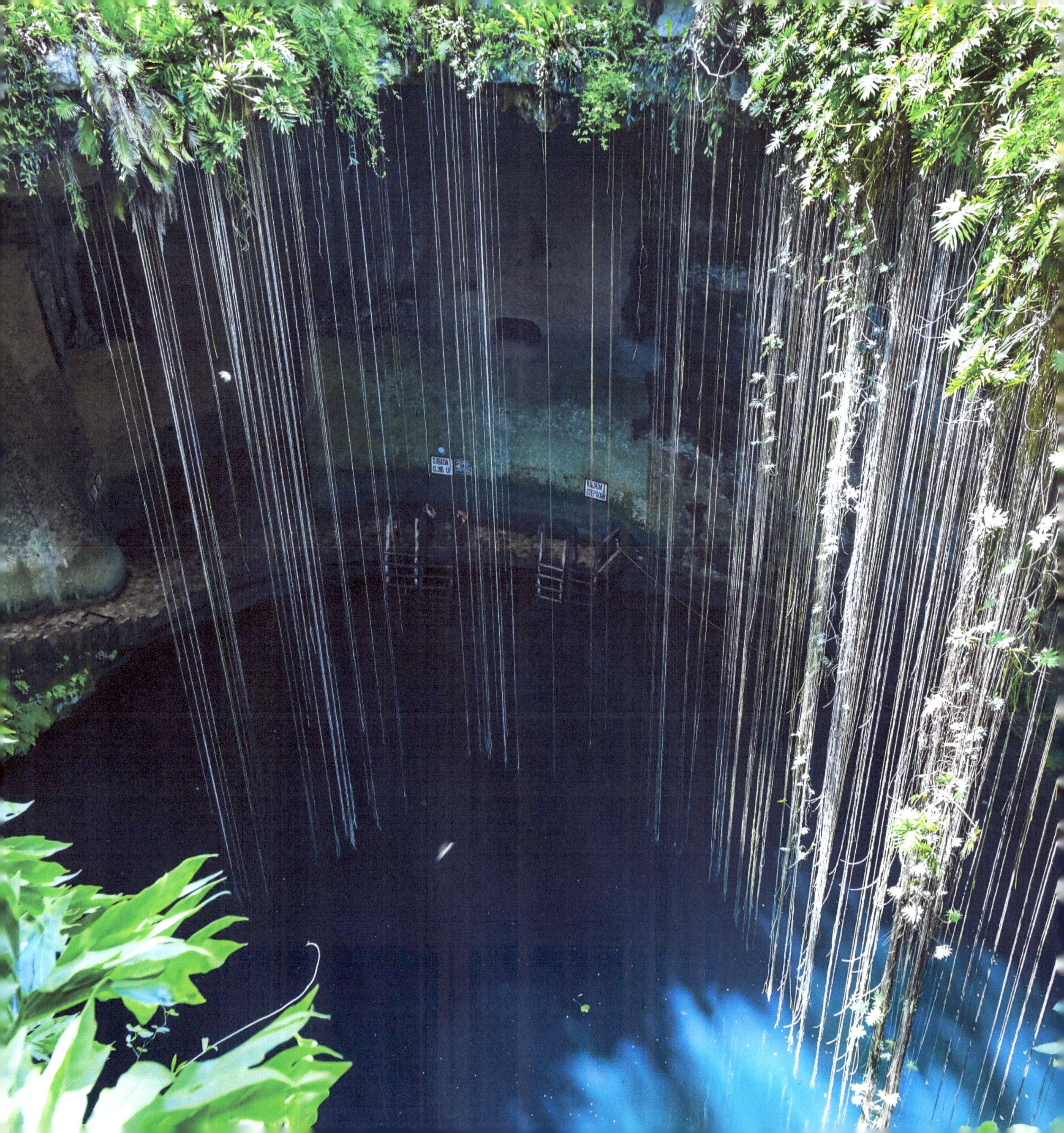
SUBIDA
CLIMB-UP
BAJADA
STEPDOWN

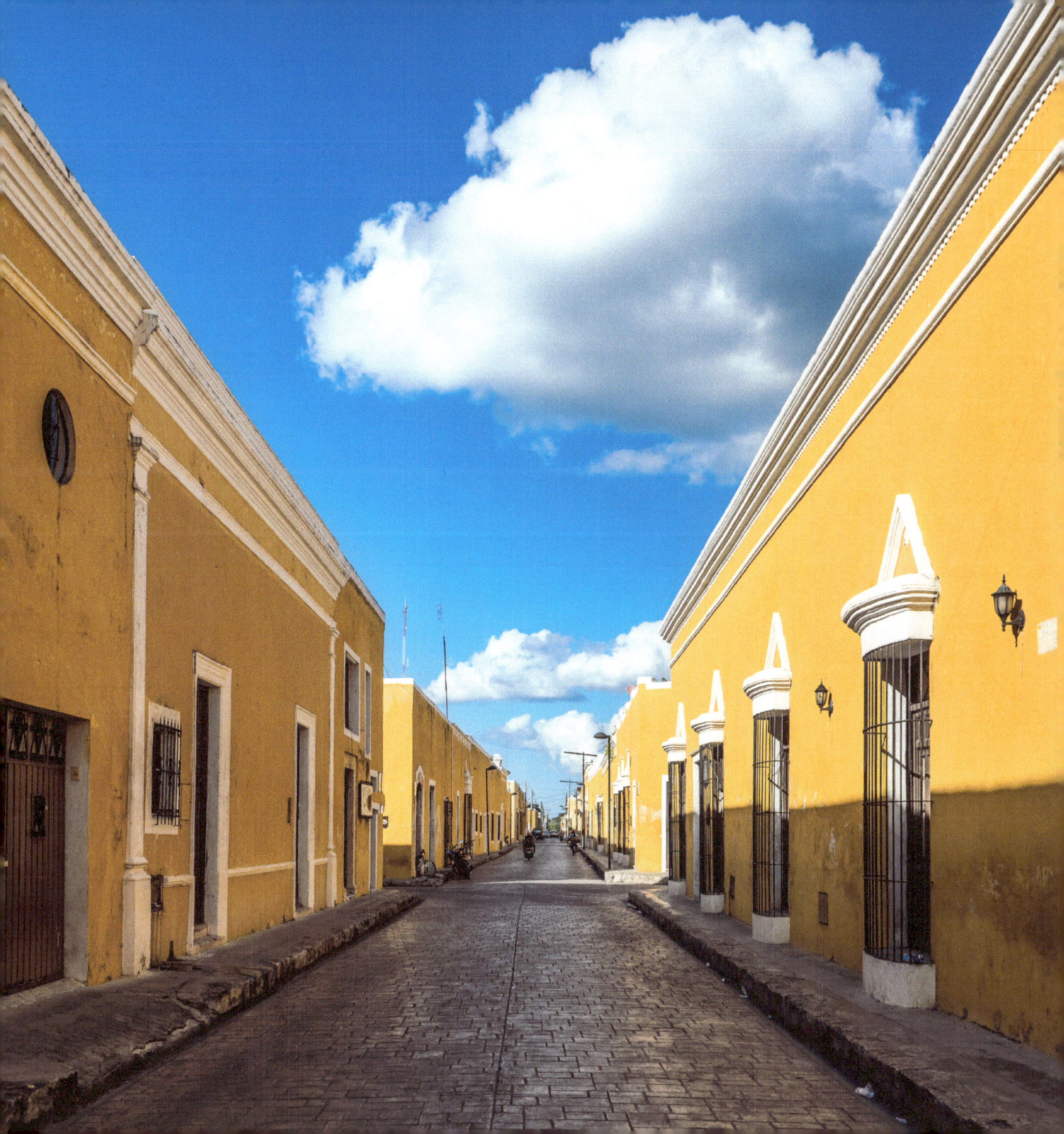

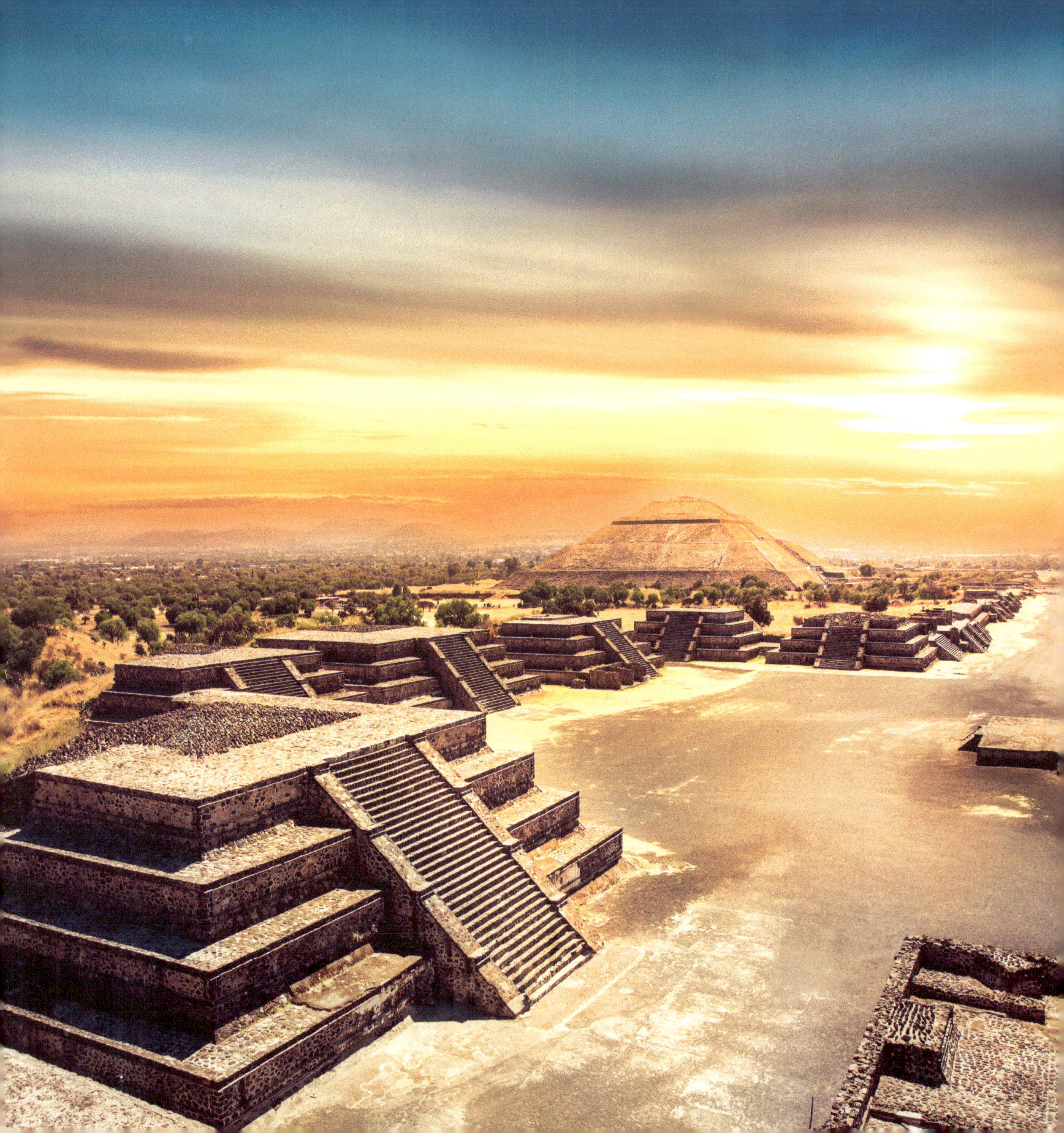

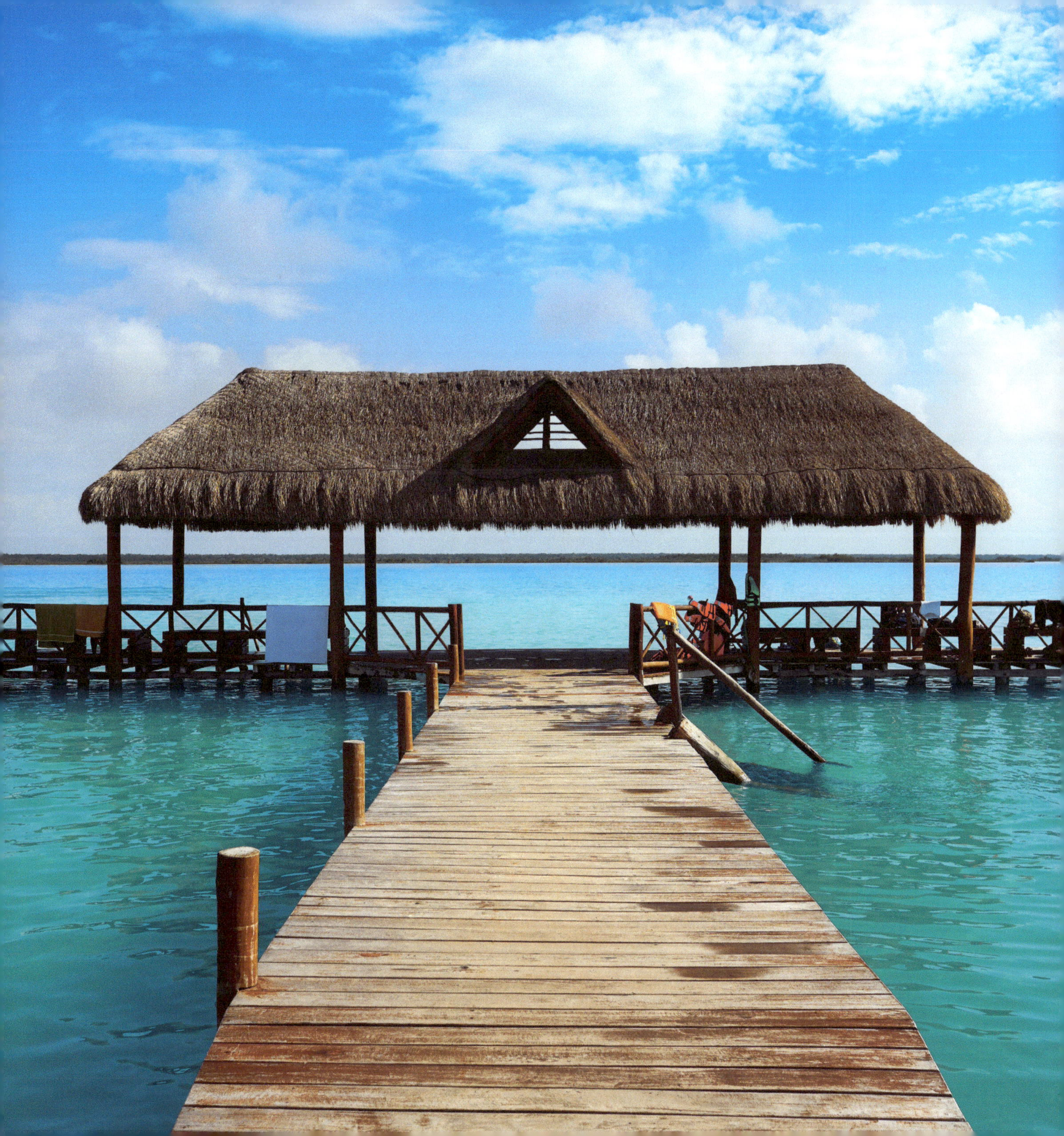

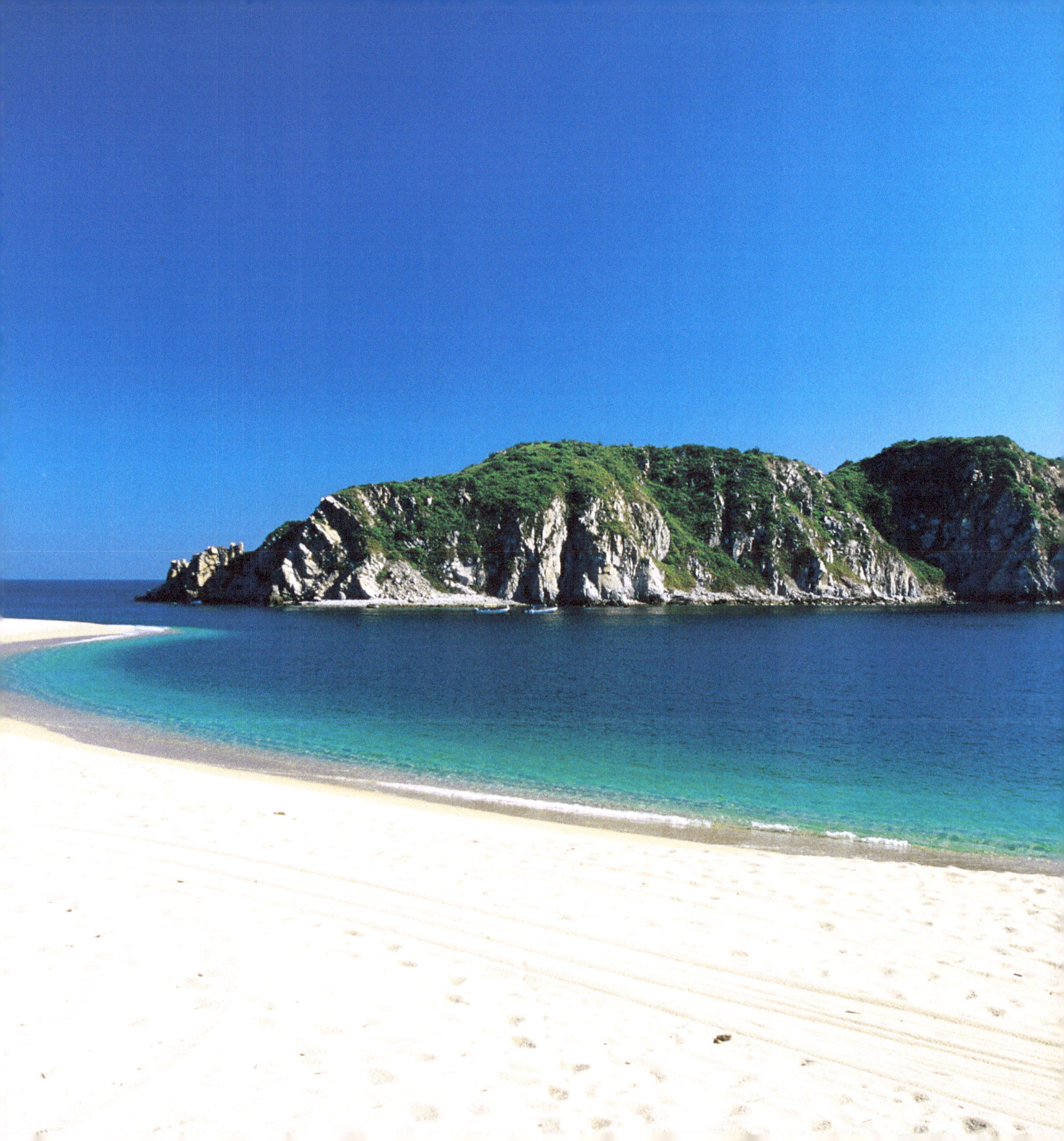

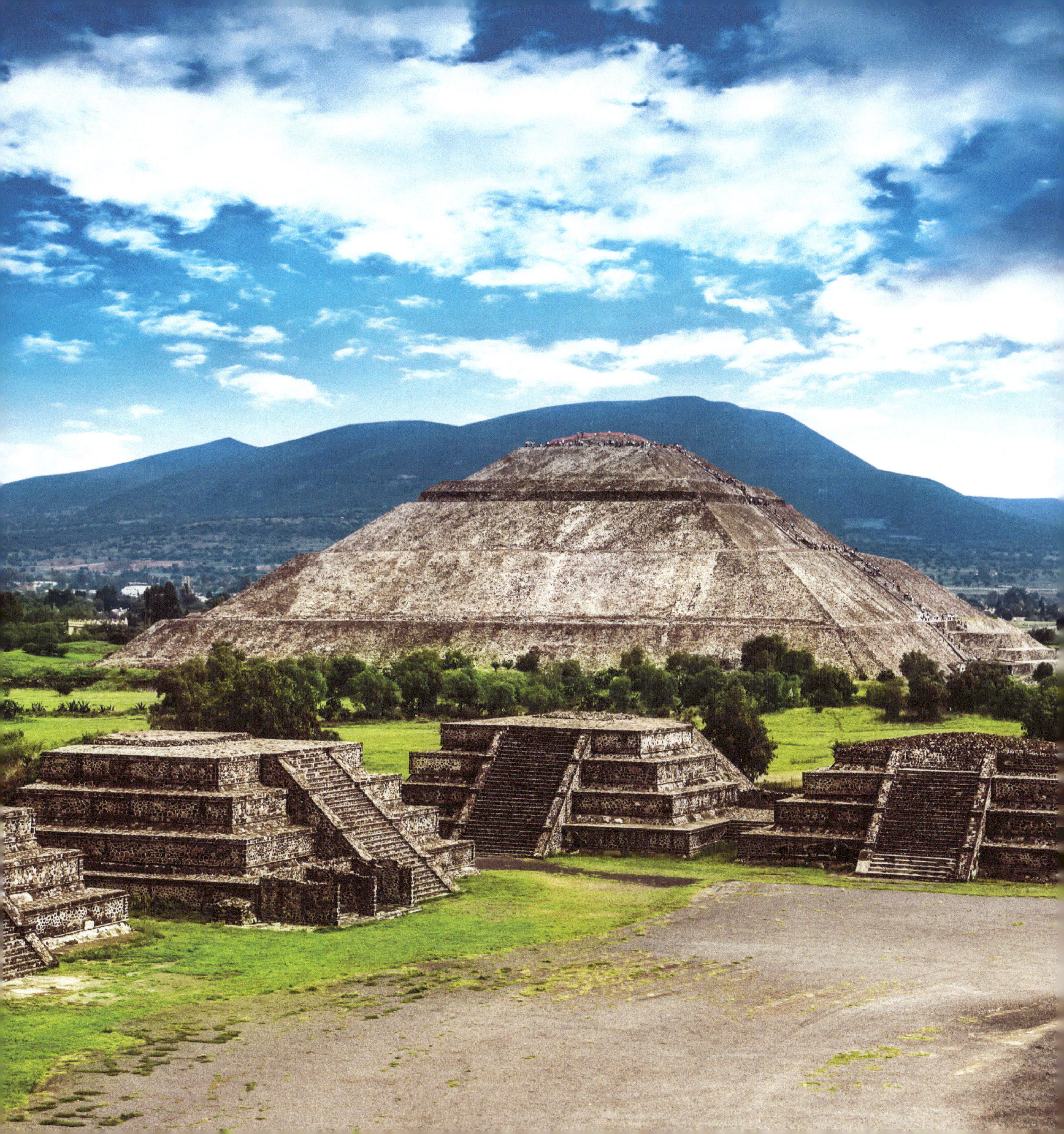

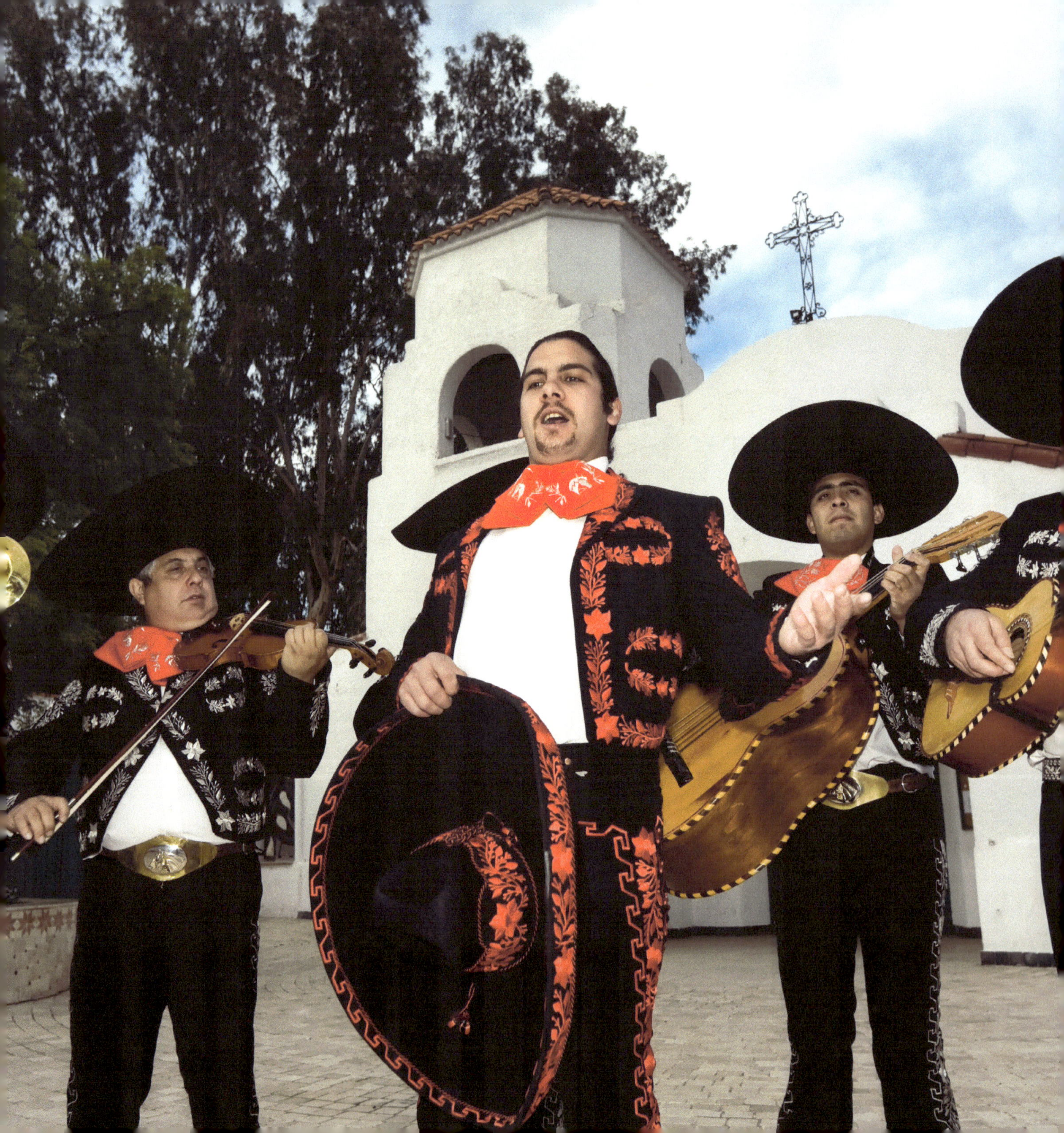

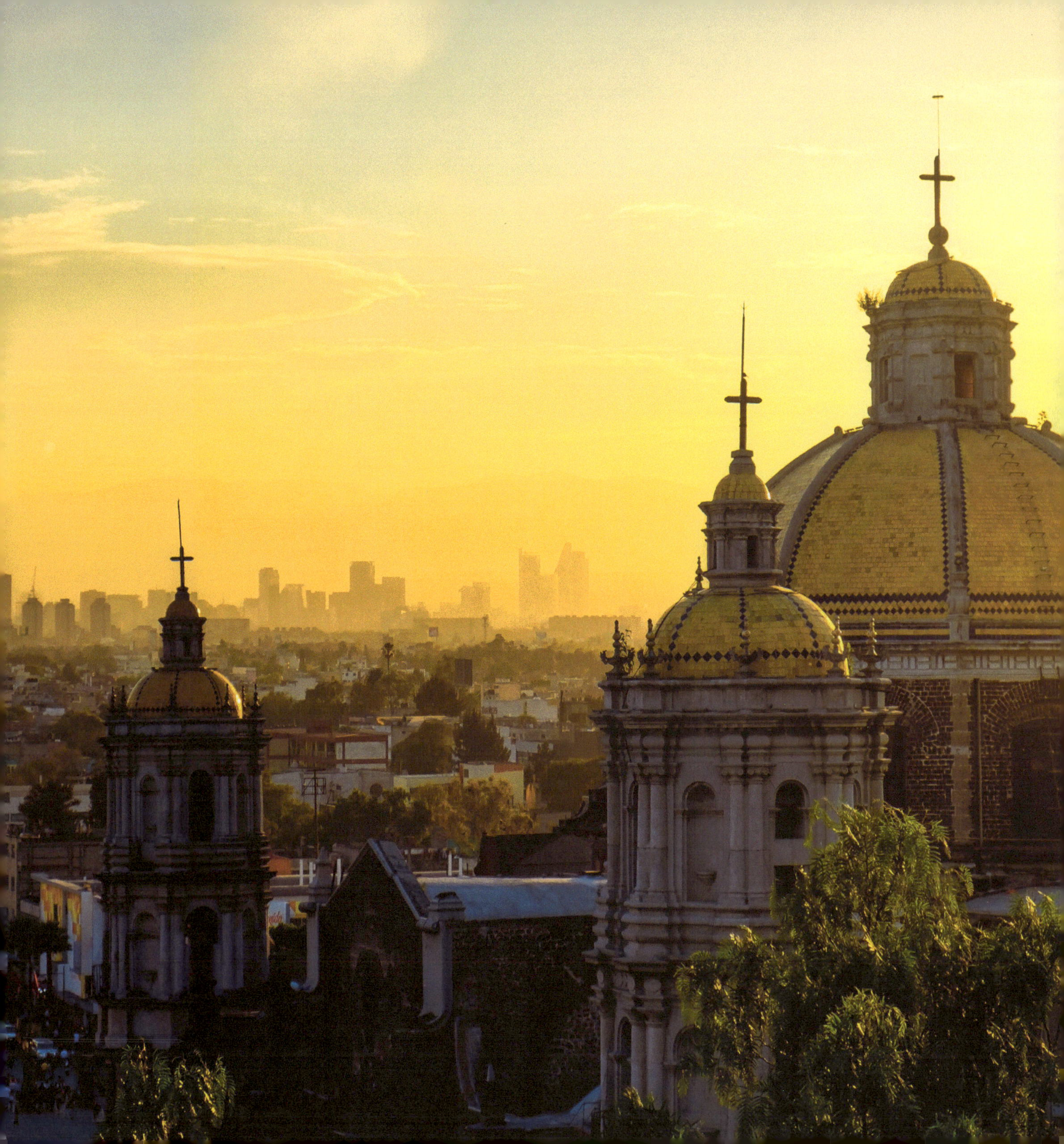

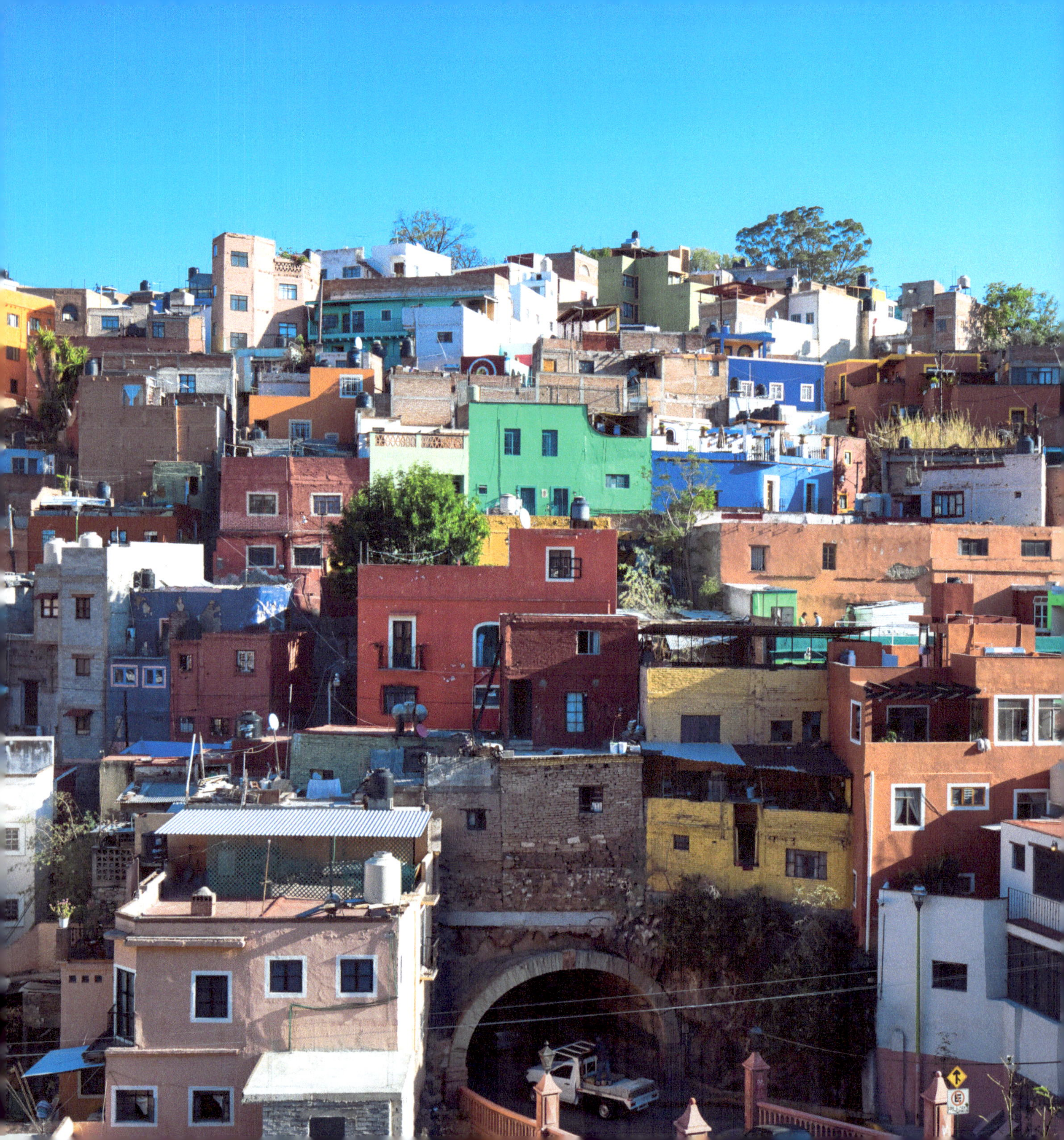

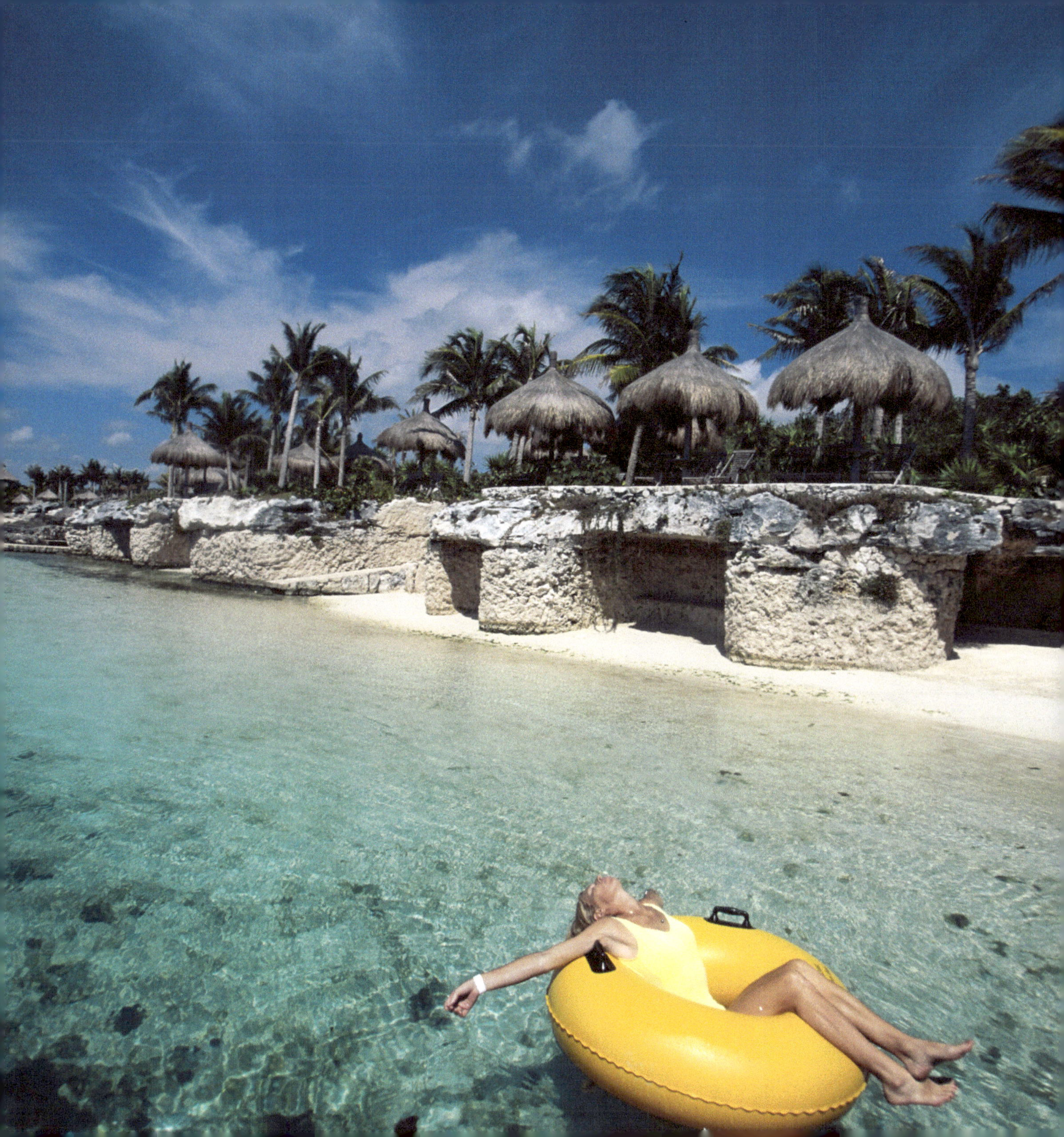

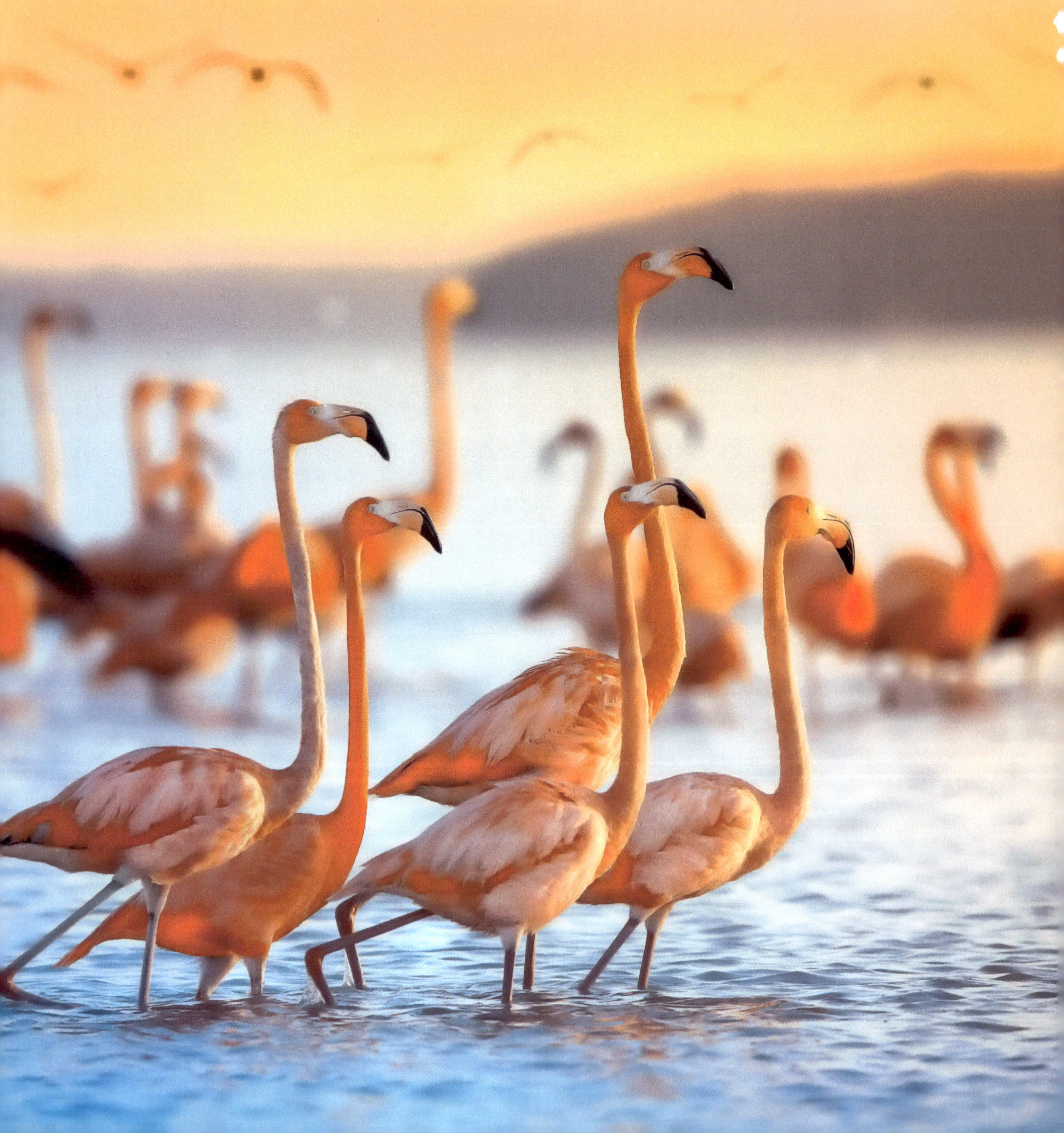

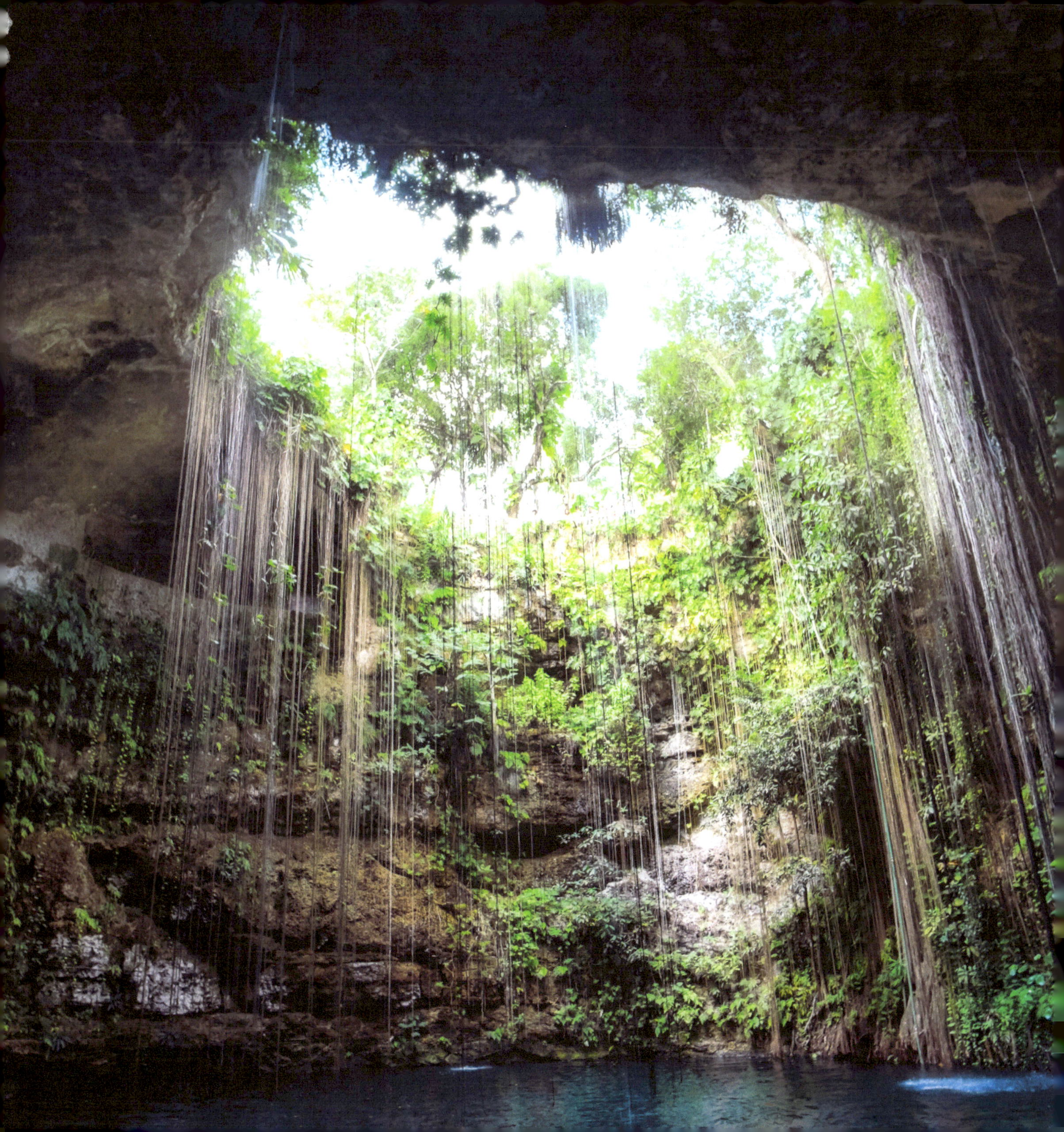

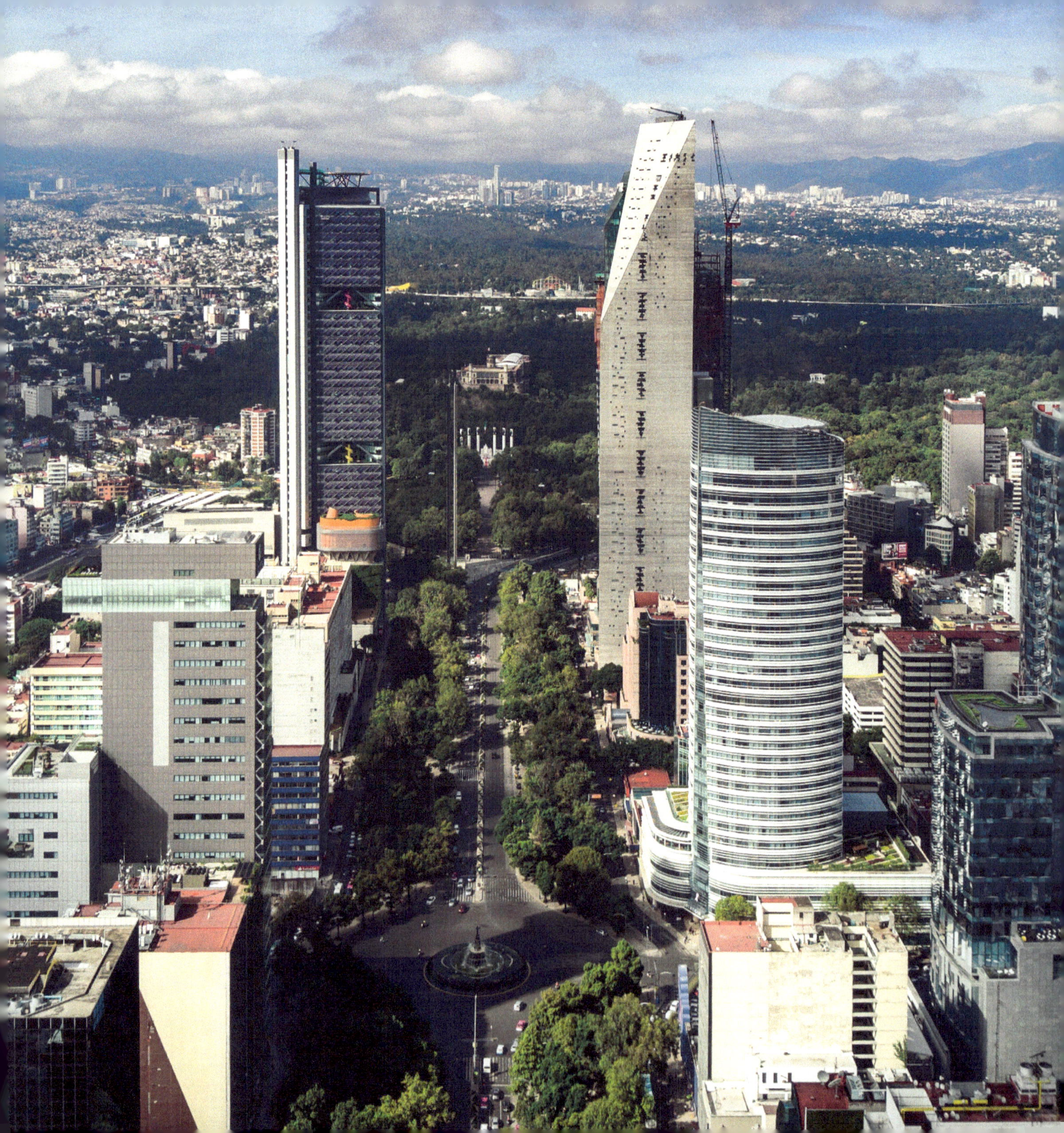

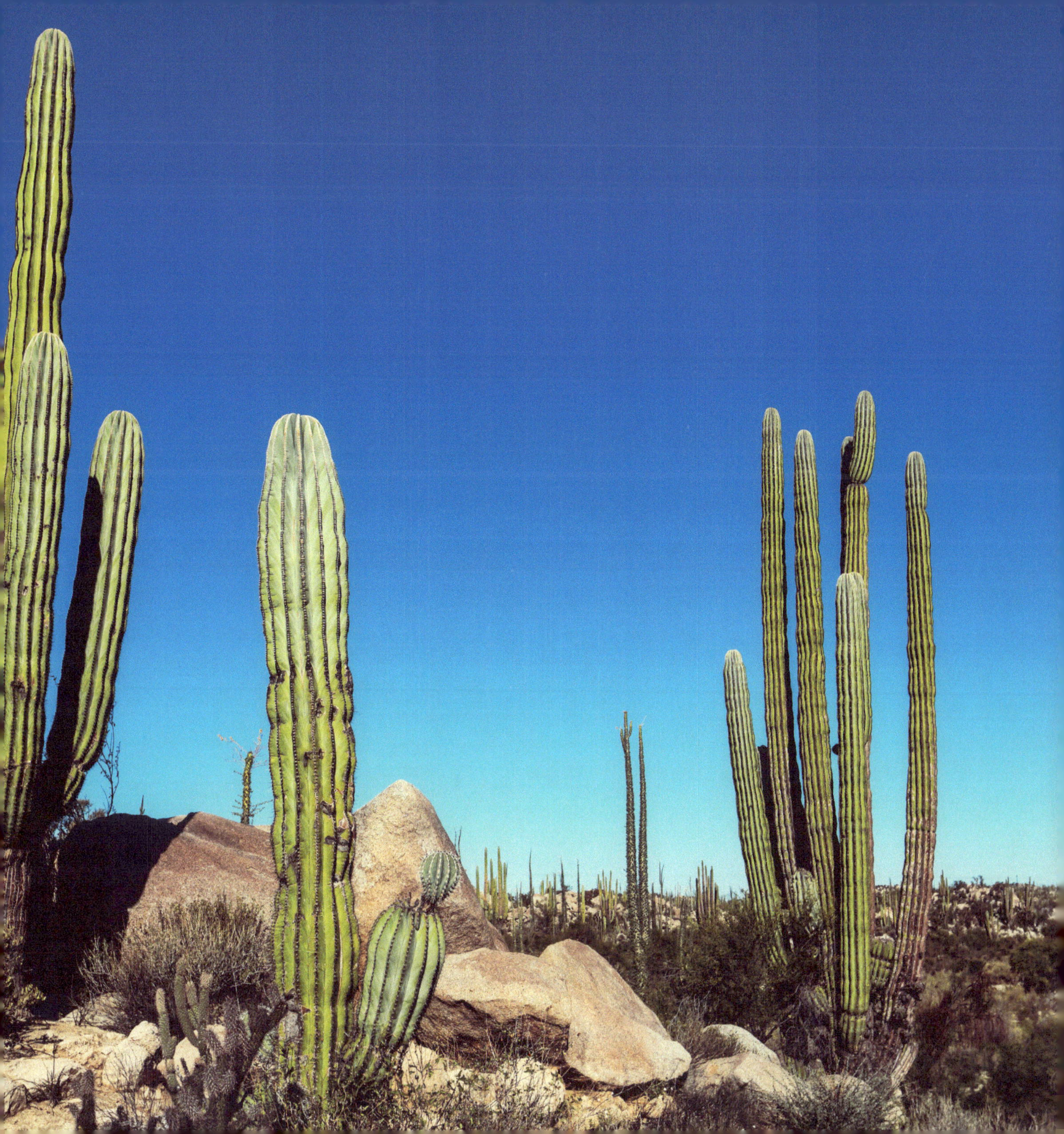

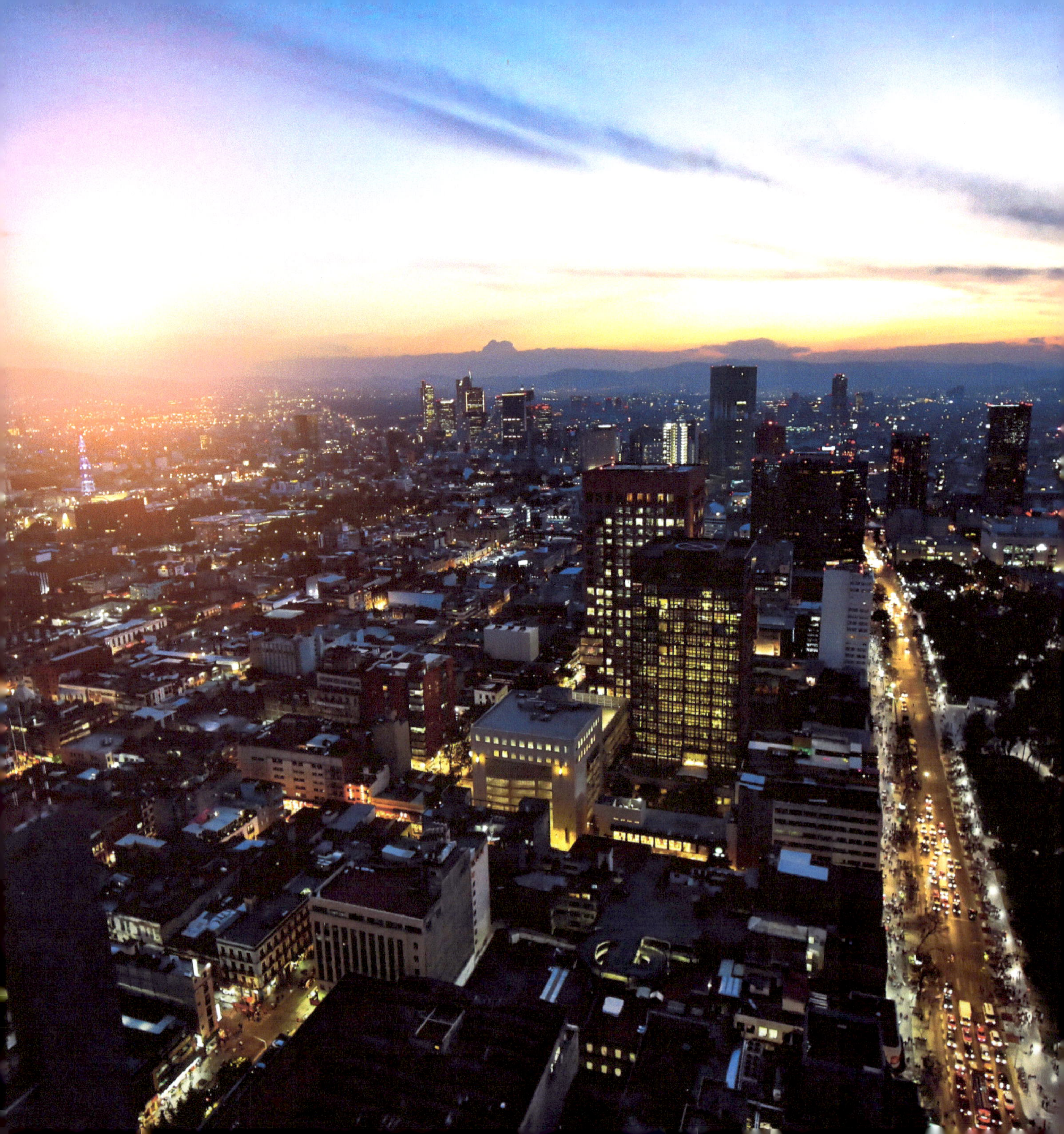

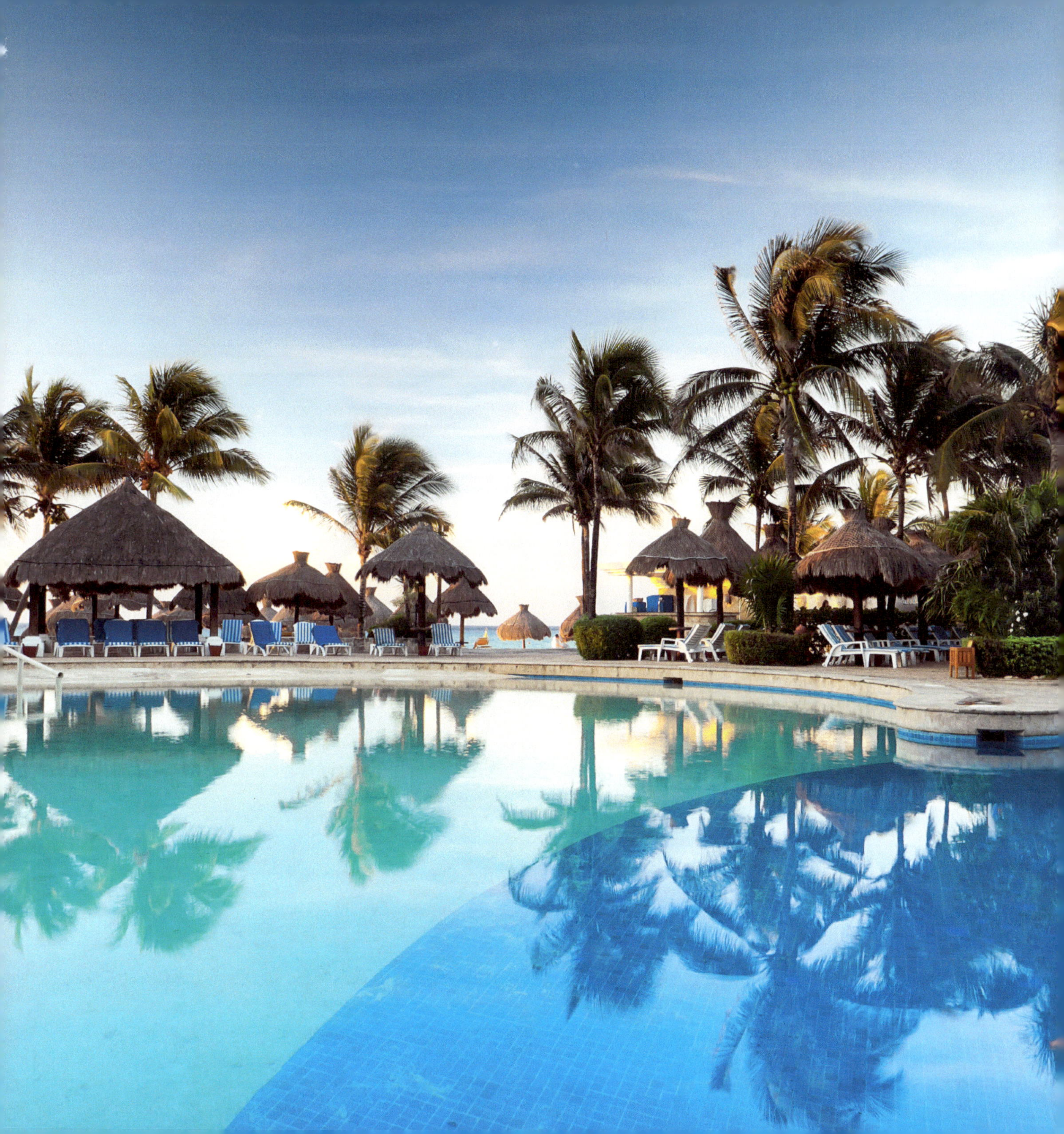

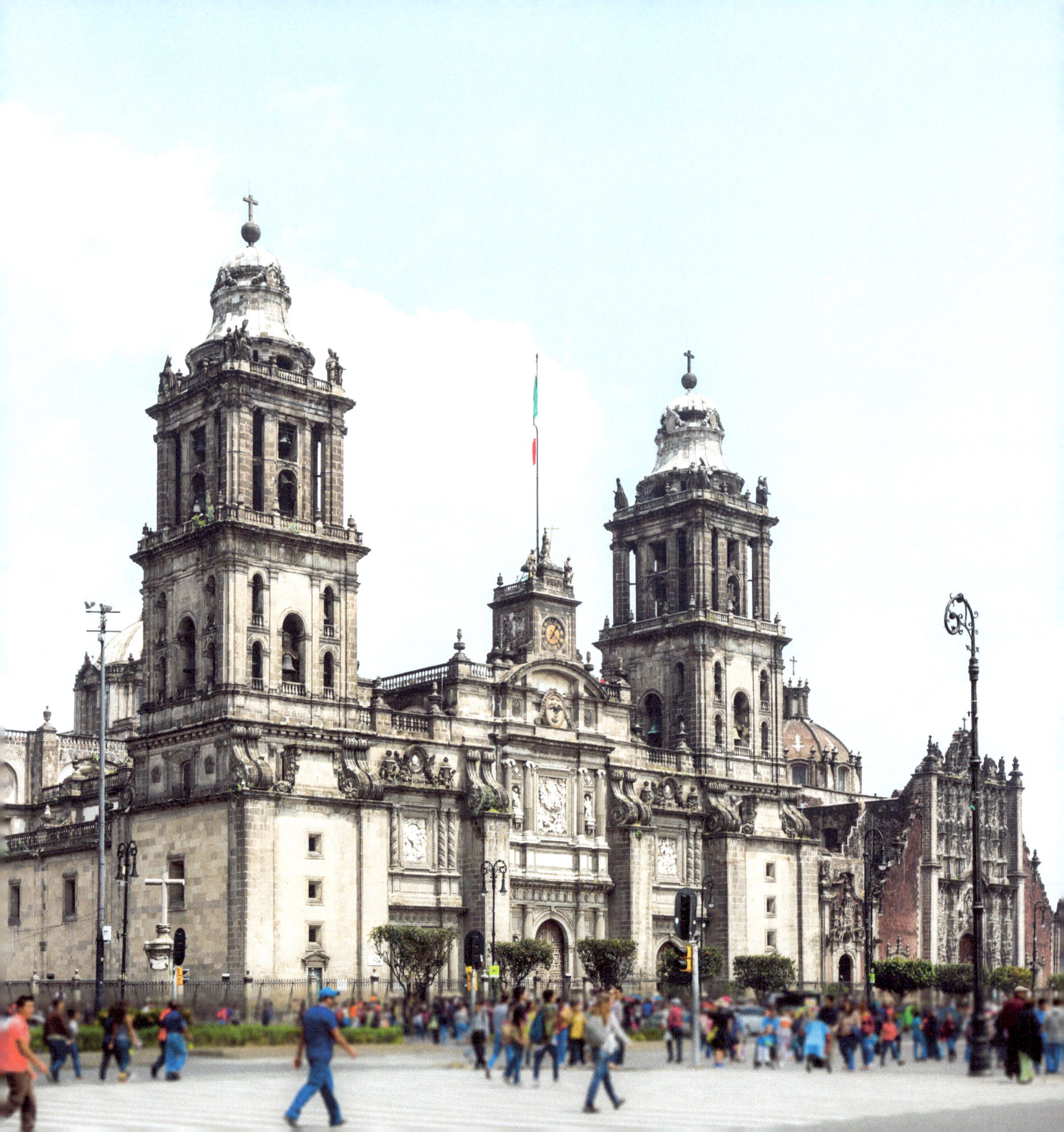

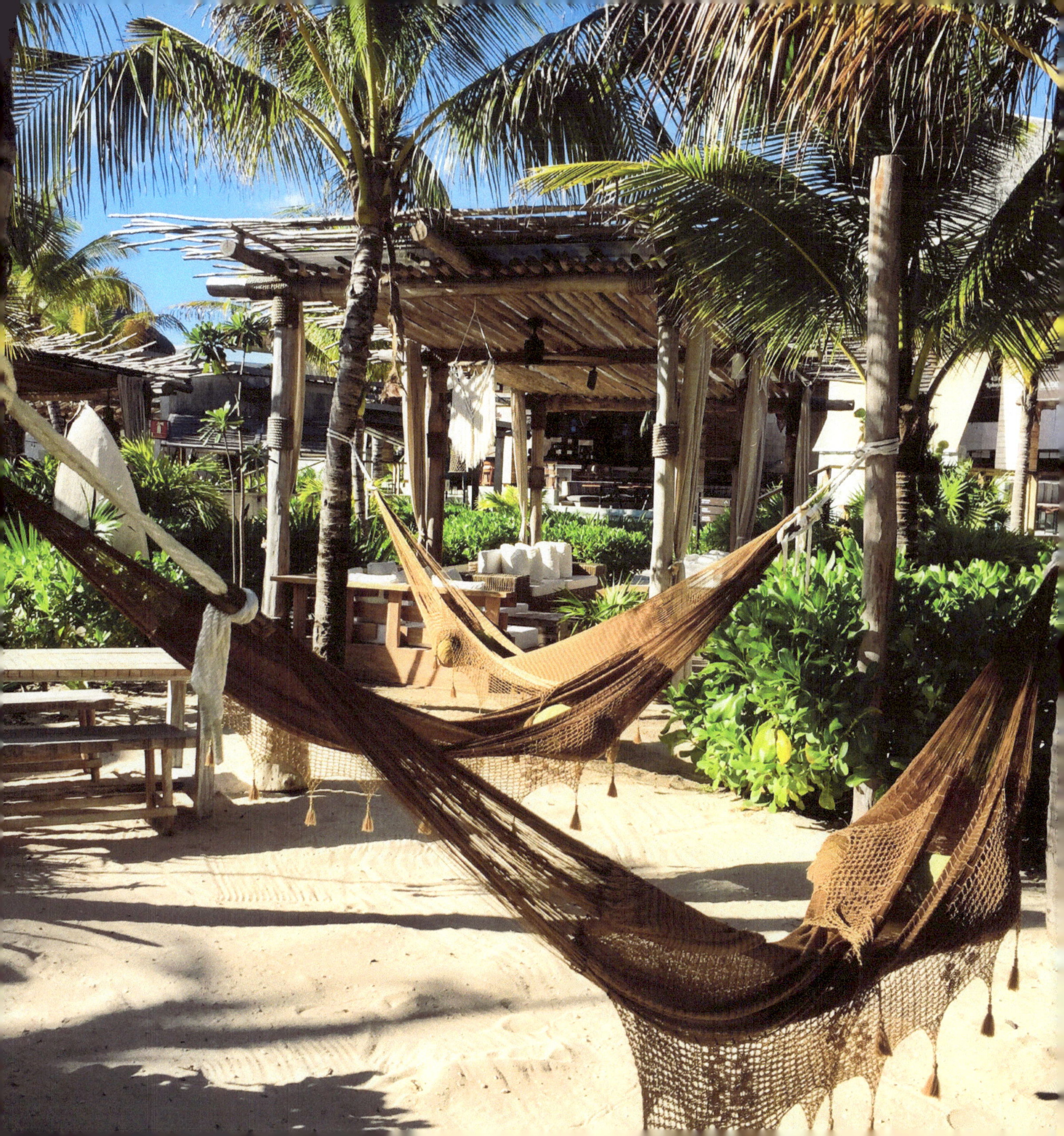

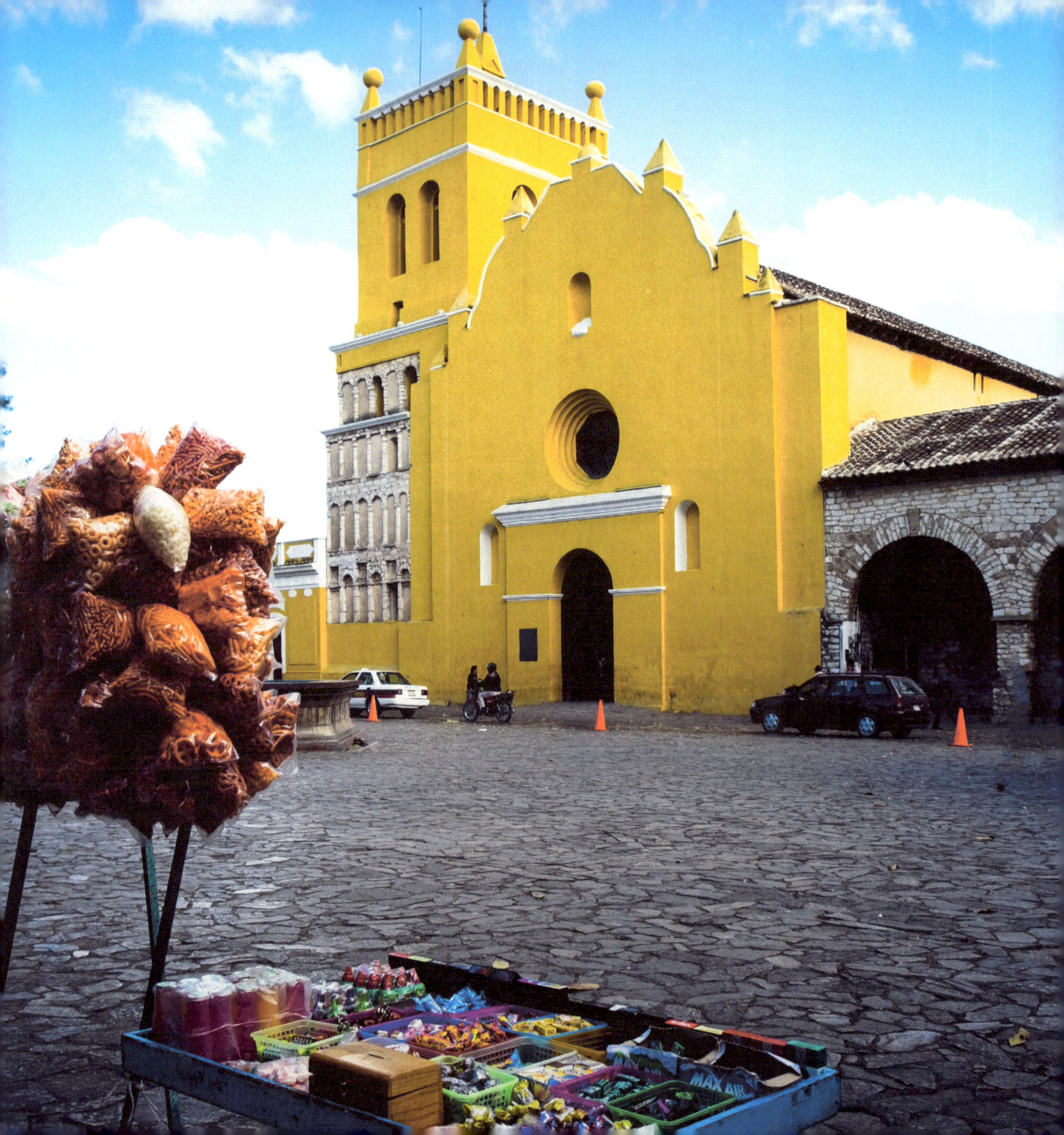
MAX AIR

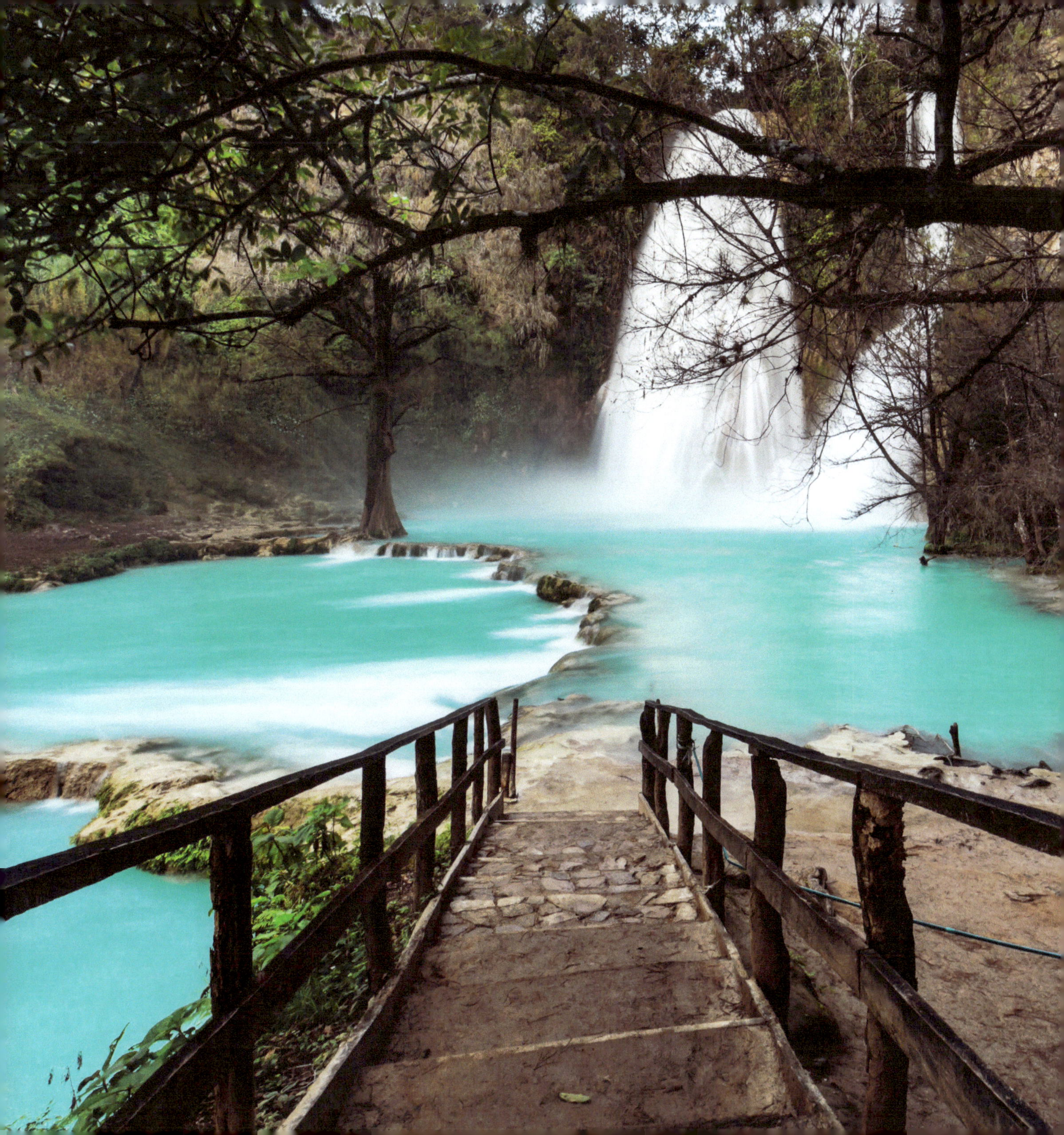

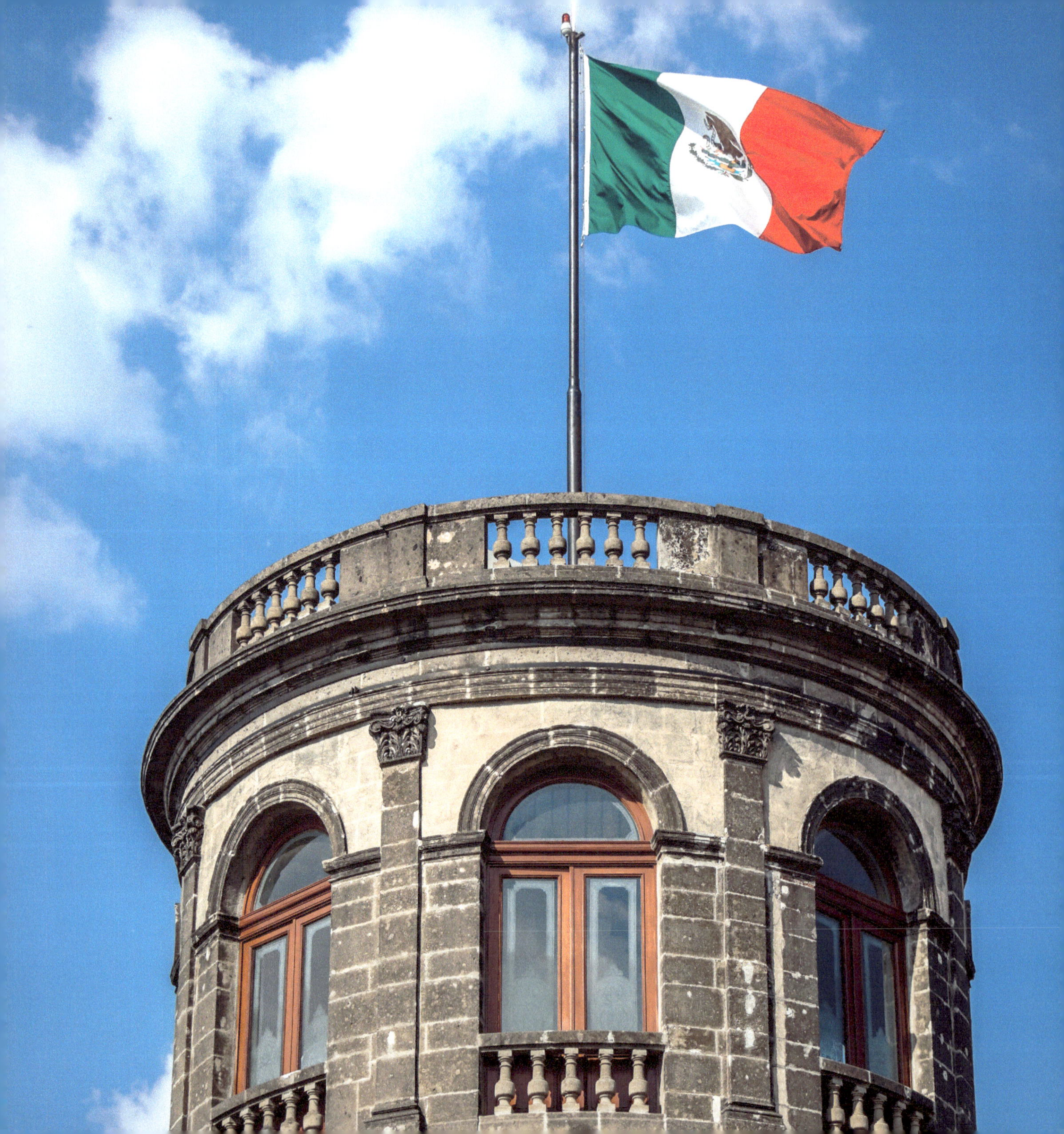

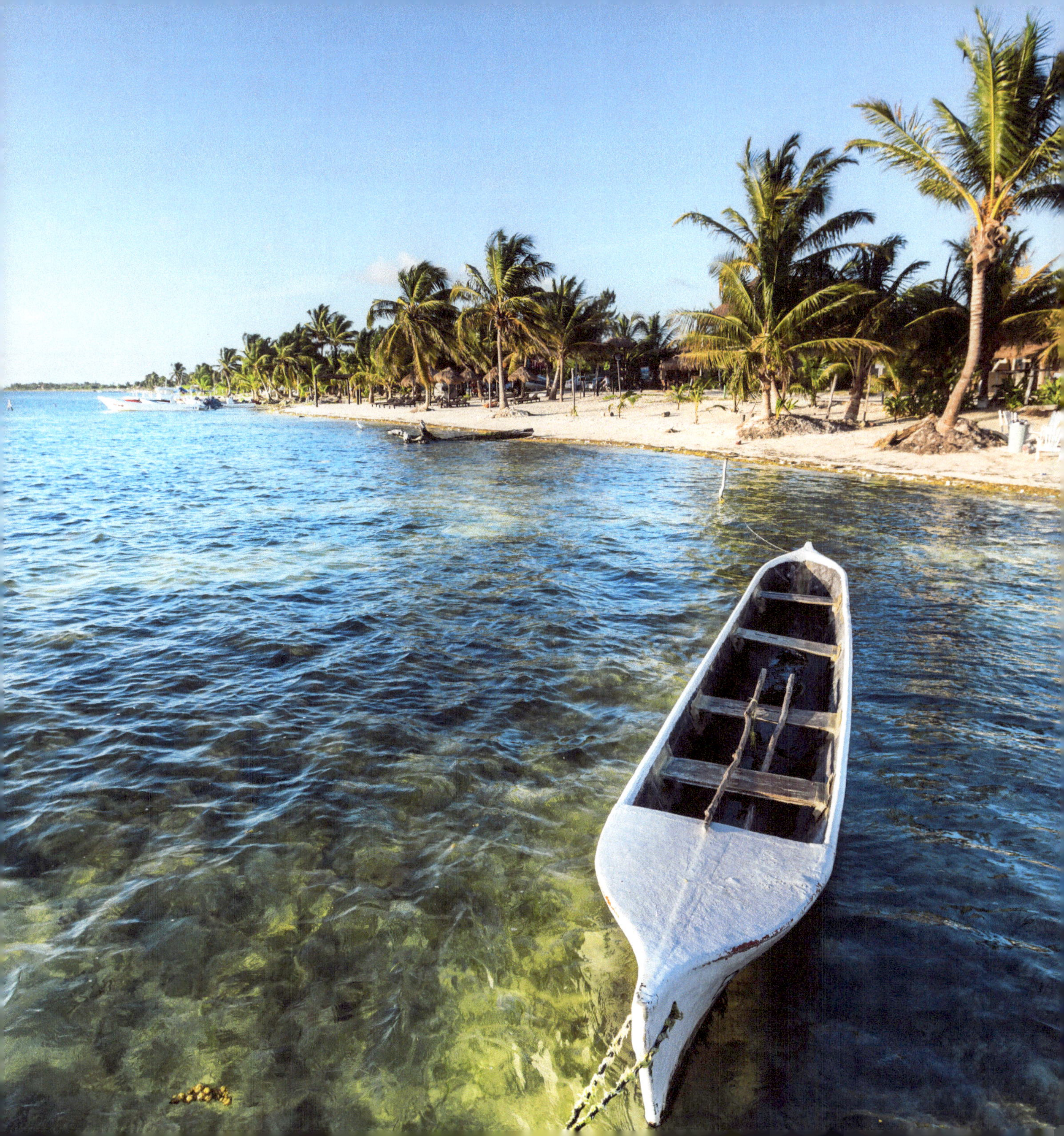

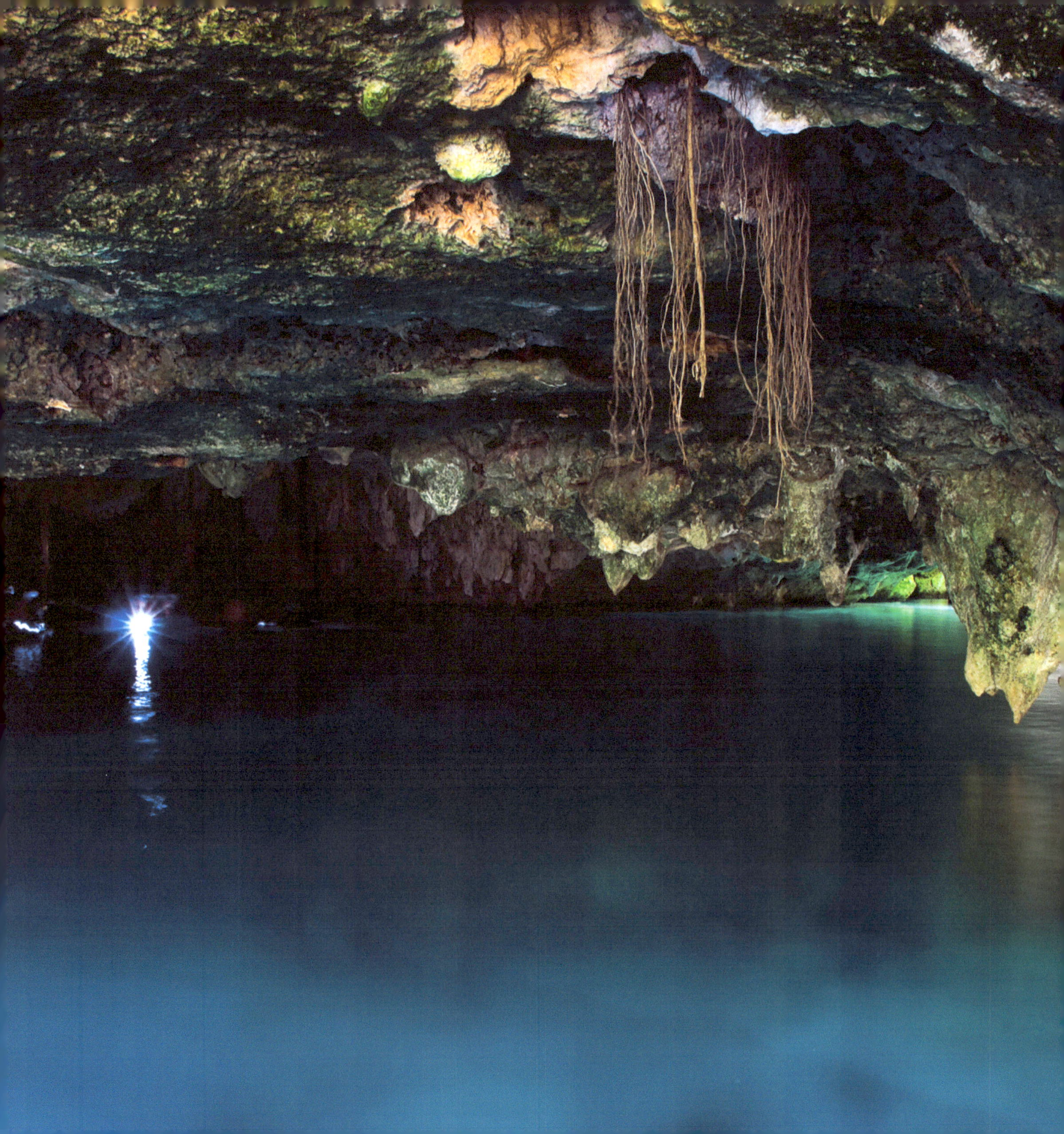

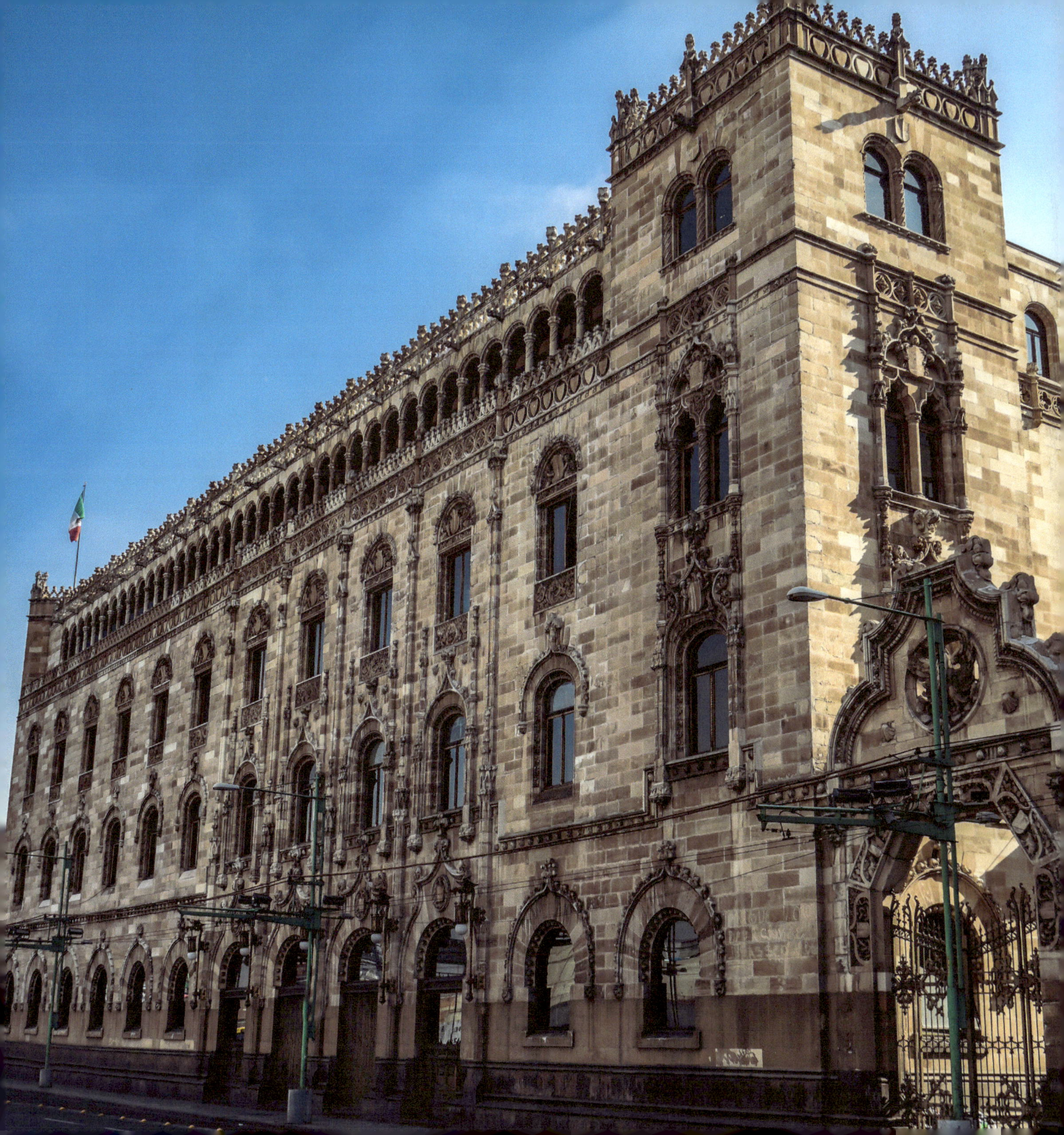

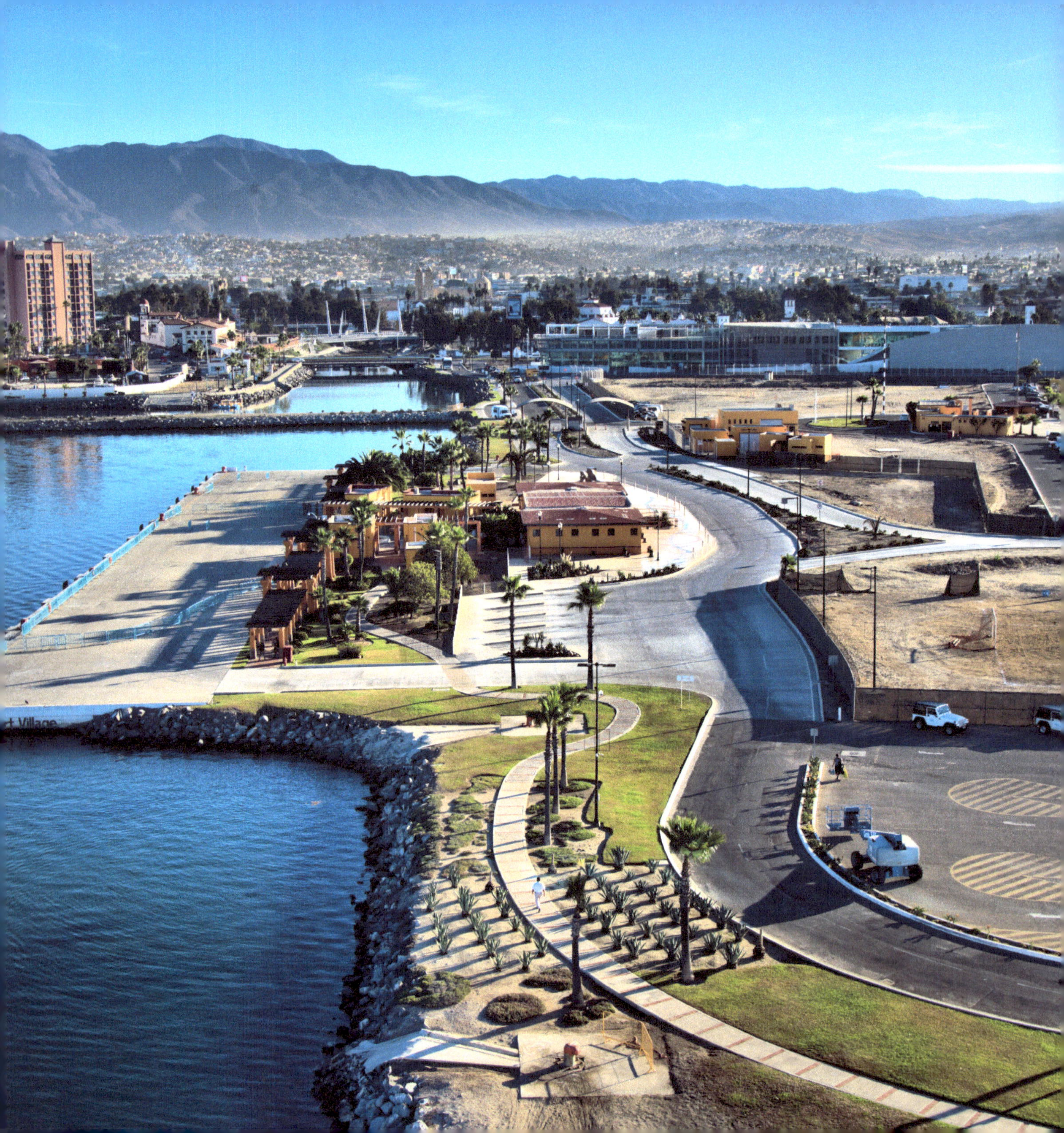
t Village

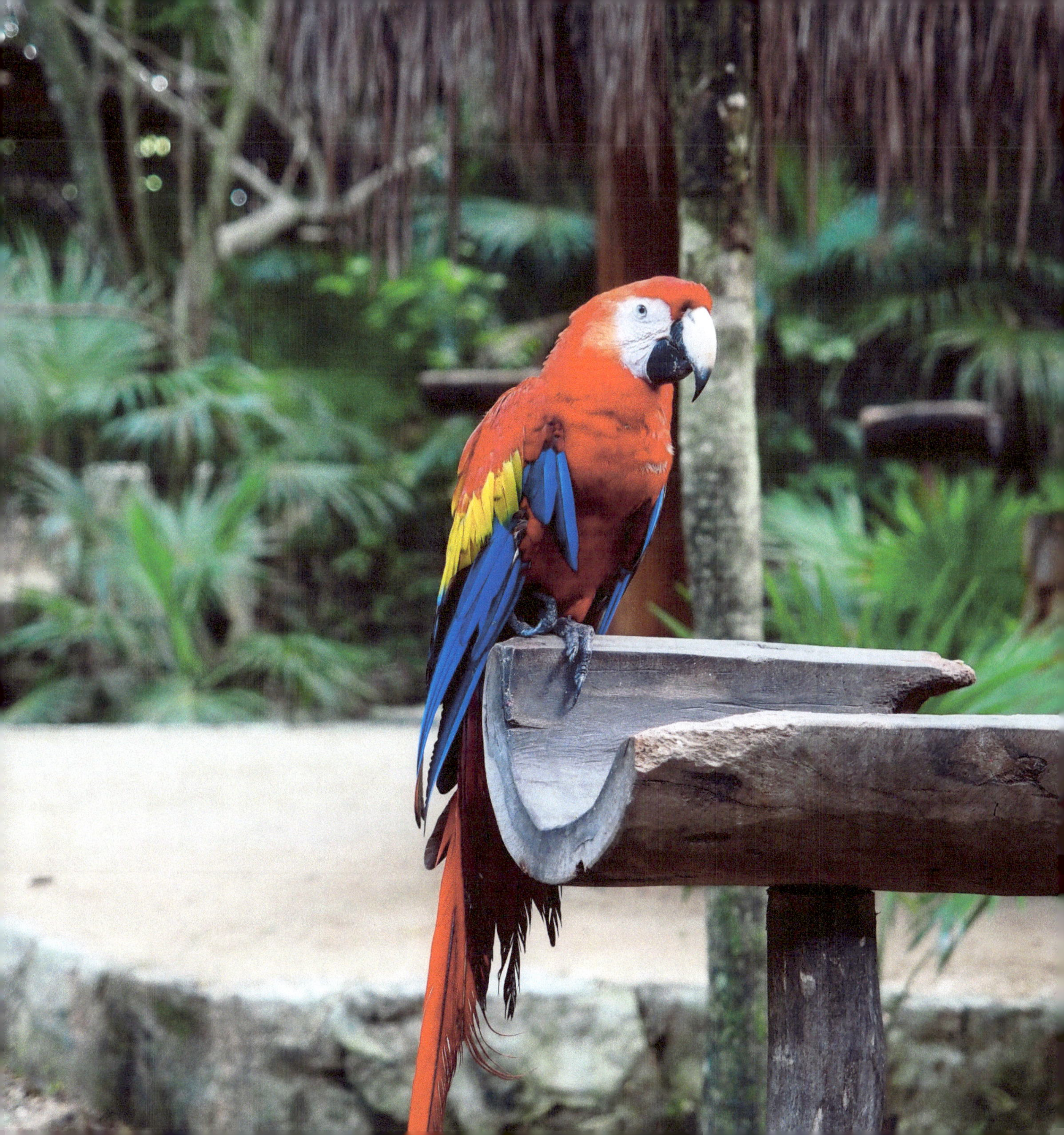

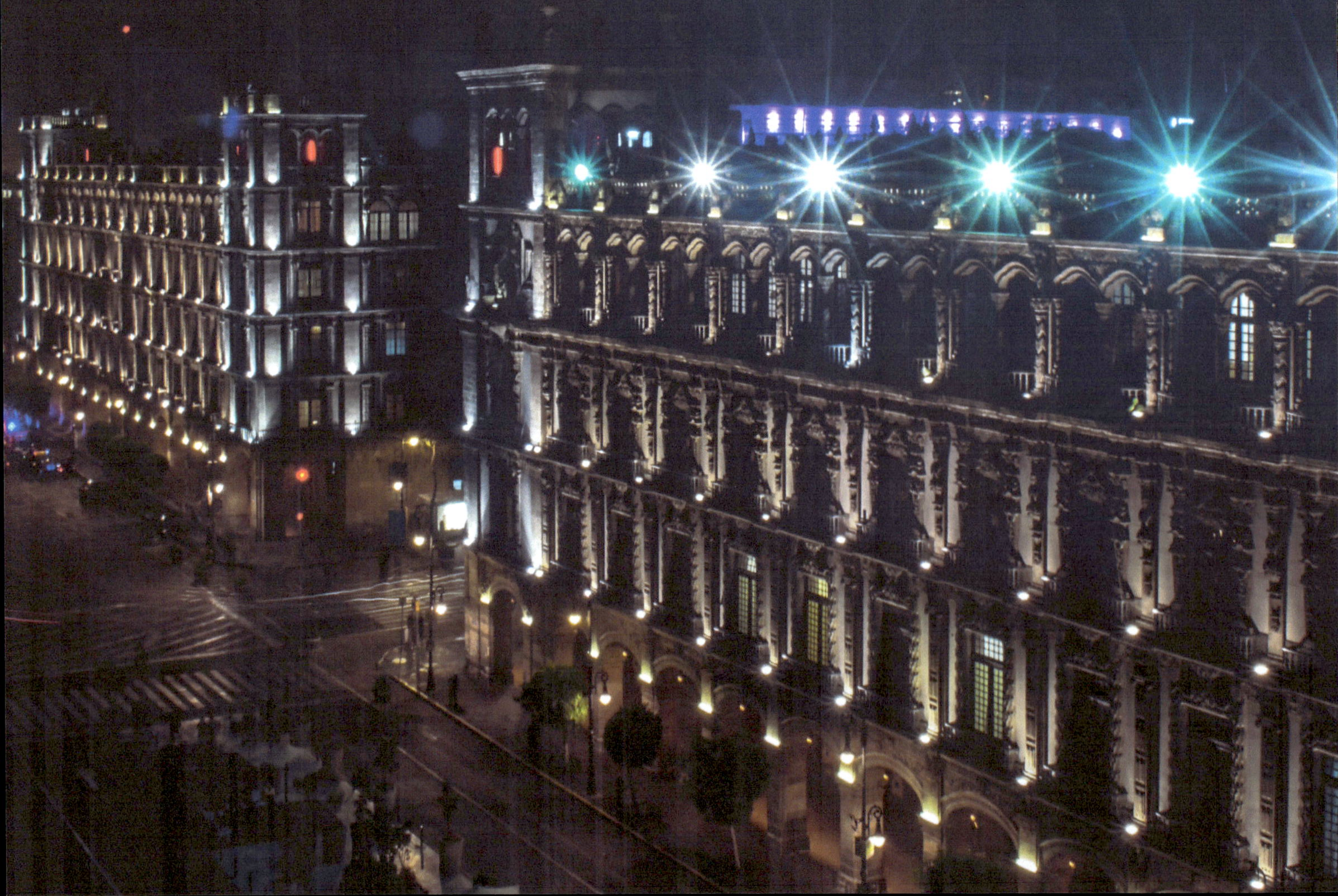

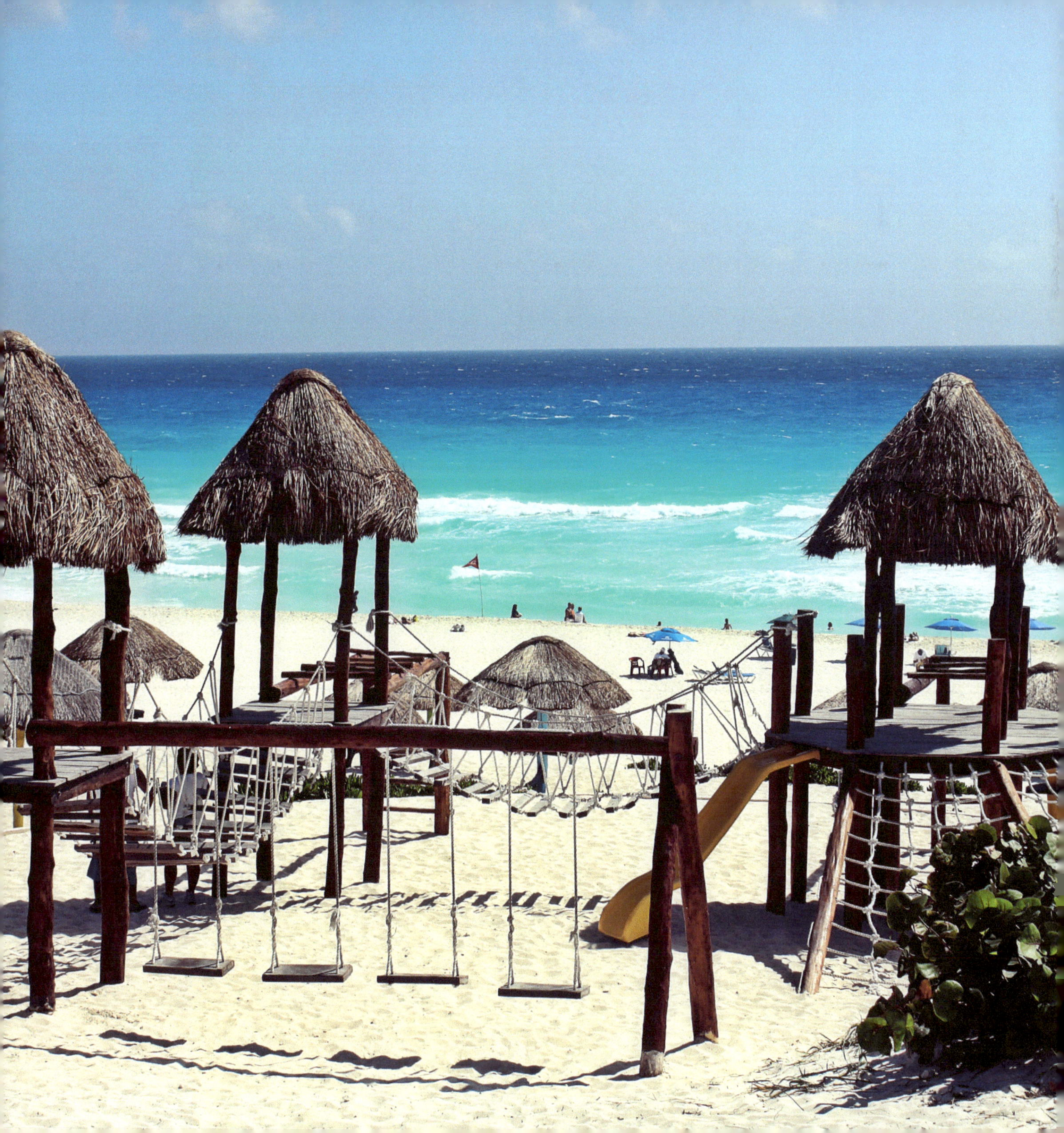

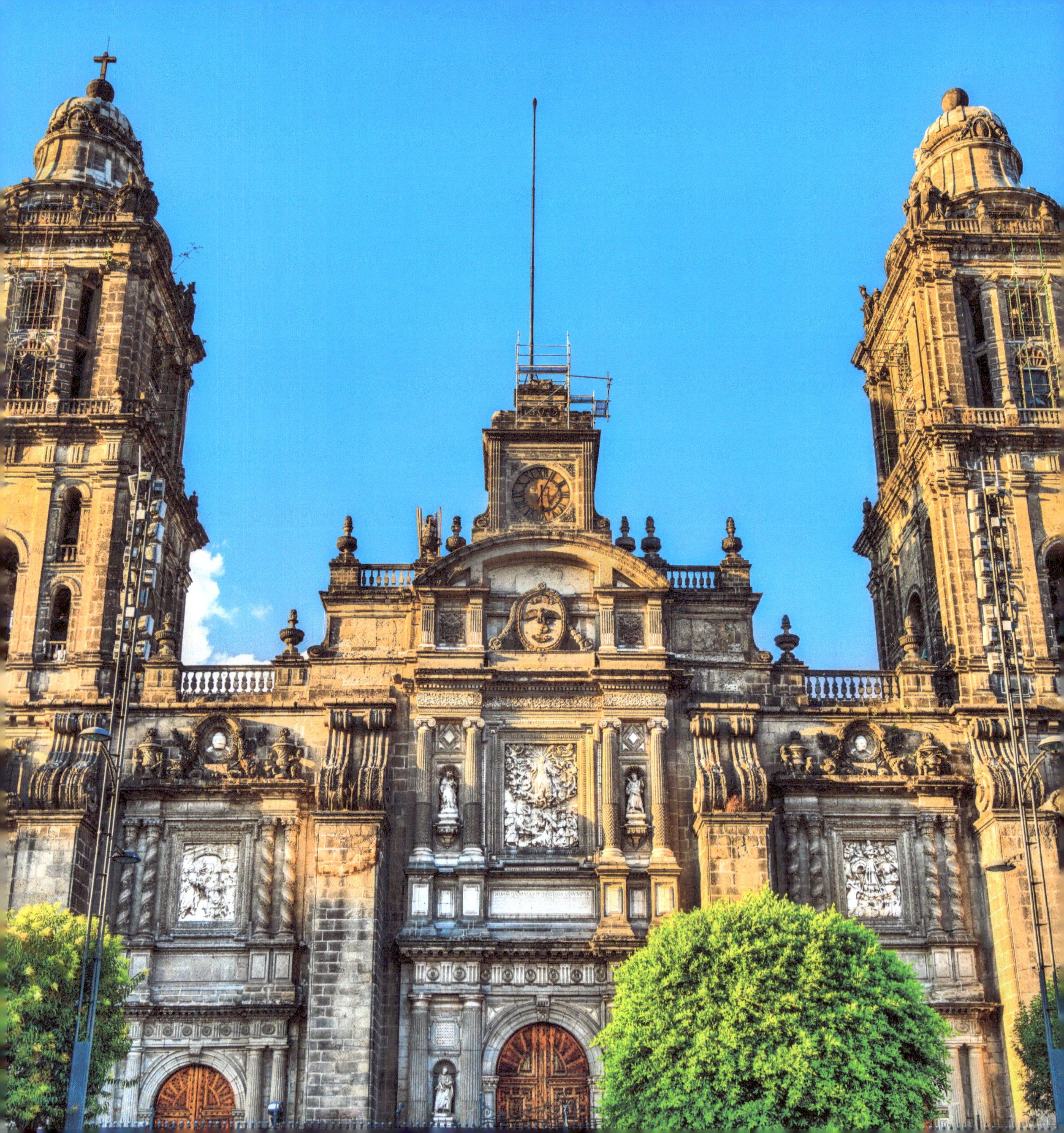

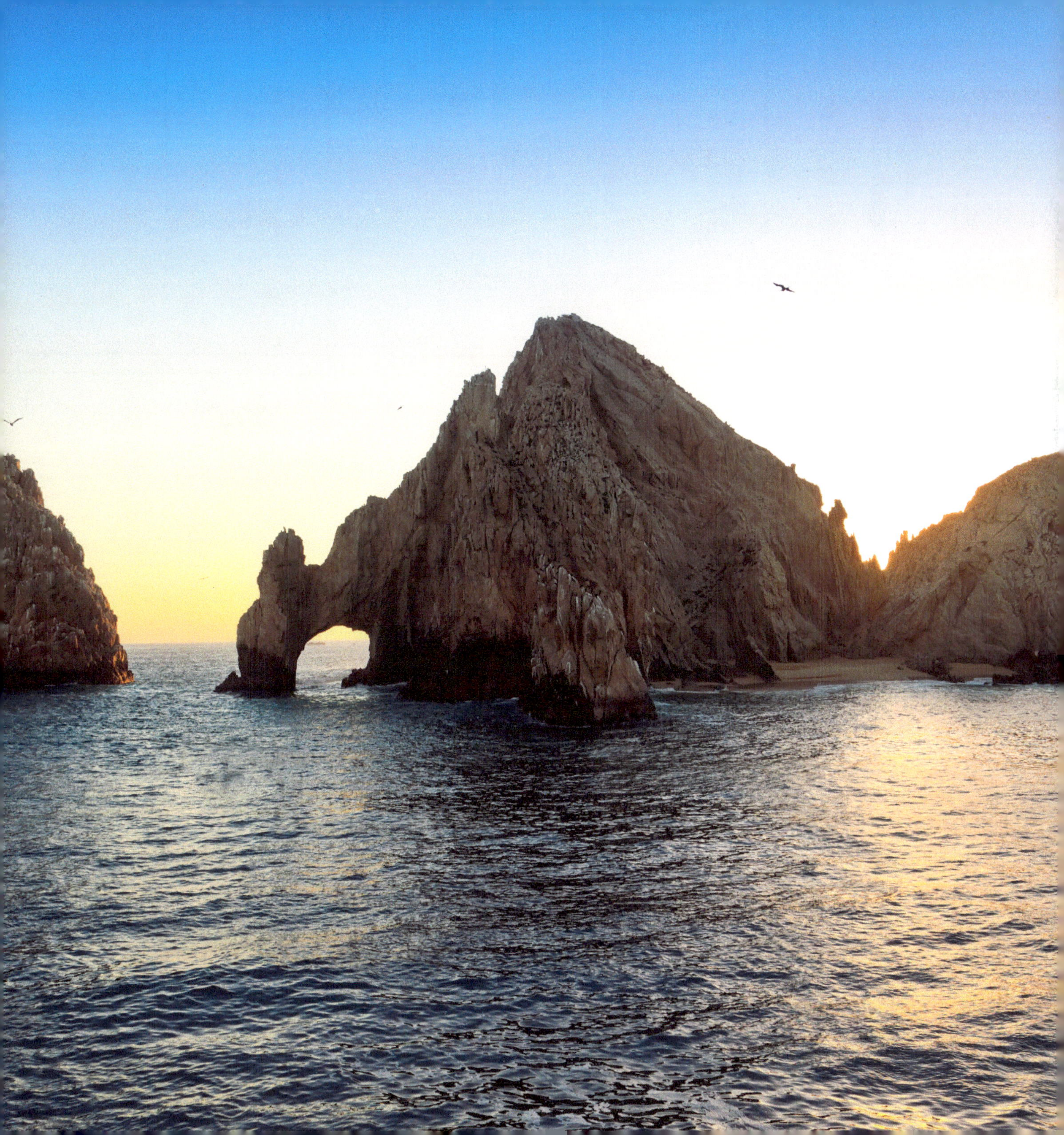

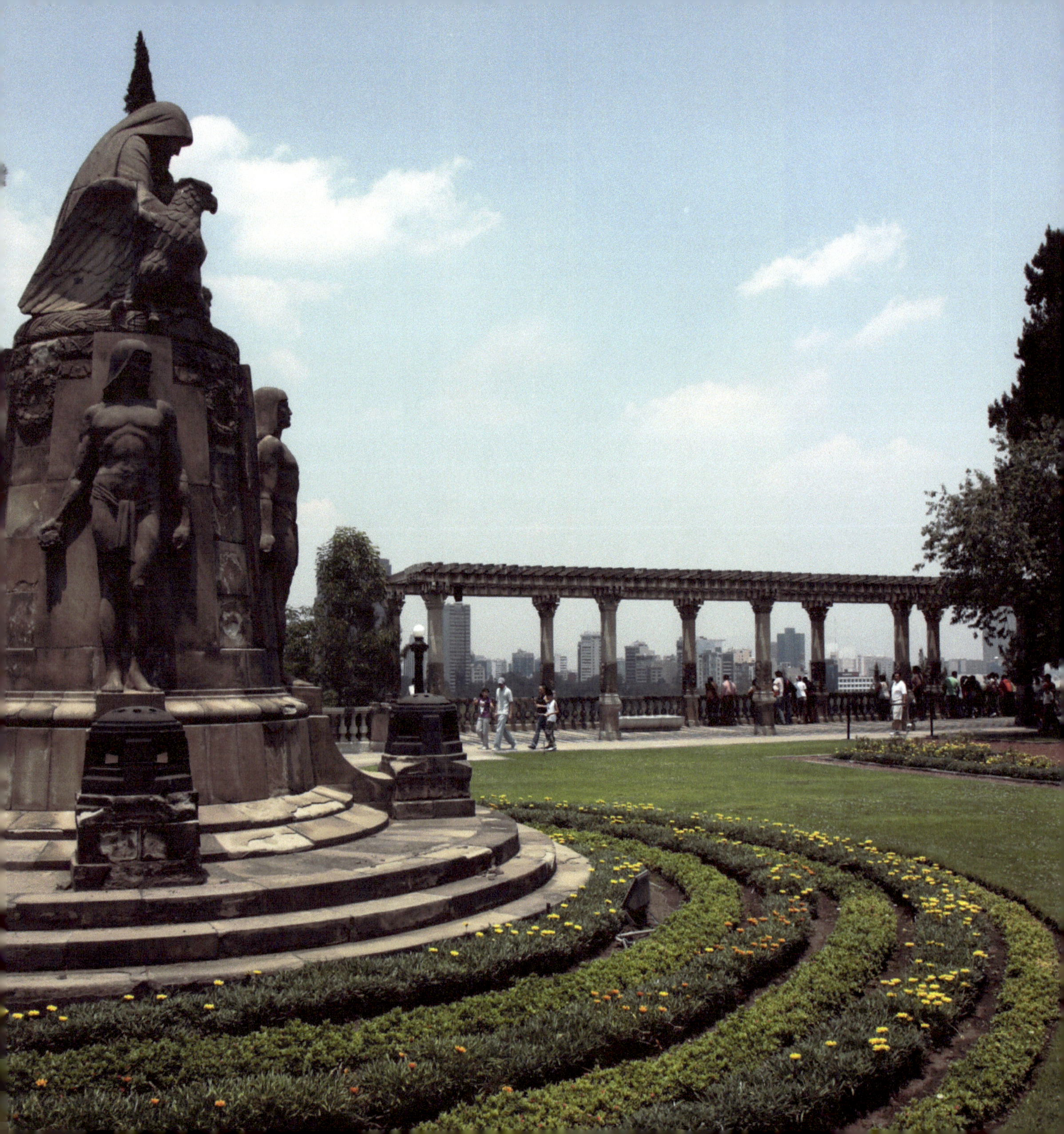

www.ingramcontent.com/pod-product-compliance
Lightning Source LLC
Chambersburg PA
CBHW040418220526
45473CB00004B/1276
* 9 7 9 8 4 2 1 5 8 7 6 7 5 *